Modern Chinese

Modern Chinese

A BASIC COURSE

by the Faculty of

PEKING UNIVERSITY

Dover Publications, Inc.
New York

Published in Canada by General Publishing
Company, Ltd., 30 Lesmill Road, Don Mills,
Toronto, Ontario.
Published in the United Kingdom by Constable
and Company, Ltd., 10 Orange Street, London WC 2.

This Dover edition, first published in 1971, is a
revised republication of the Introduction and the
first thirty lessons from the second, 1963, edition of
Modern Chinese Reader, originally published by
the "Epoch" Publishing House, Peking (first edition:
1958).
This book is sold separately, and also as part of a
package (entitled *Modern Chinese: A Basic Course*)
which also contains three 12-inch long-playing
records (Dover catalog number 98832-5).
The Publisher's note to this English edition gives
more information on the records and further
bibliographic details.

International Standard Book Number
(text, records and album): 0-486-98832-5
International Standard Book Number
(text only): 0-486-22755-3
Library of Congress Catalog Card Number: 78-169835

Manufactured in the United States of America
Dover Publications, Inc.
180 Varick Street
New York, N. Y. 10014

PUBLISHER'S NOTE

This book contains the Introduction and the first thirty lessons of *Modern Chinese Reader* (second edition, Peking, 1963), which was compiled by the instructors of the Chinese Language Special Course for Foreign Students in Peking University.*

It was felt that these first thirty lessons comprise an excellent self-contained introduction to Mandarin Chinese as it is spoken in Mainland China today. The first twelve lessons deal with phonetics, tones and pronunciation (eight theoretical and four practice lessons). The grammar lessons follow.

In the original edition, no translations were provided for any of the grammar example sentences or exercise sentences ("Texts") from Lesson 13 on. All these sentences have been translated specially for the present edition.† On the other hand, the original edition repeated all the phonetic and grammatical rules—that is, all the basic text— in Chinese, paragraph by paragraph (for the use of teachers in China). In this edition the Chinese version of this material has been omitted and only the English version is given.

The Vocabulary (glossary) appendix of the original edition has been abridged to include only the words in the first thirty lessons. The pronunciation exercises of Lessons 1 through 4 have been abridged.

The transcription system used in this book is the official one of Mainland China (see the last paragraph of the Introduction). For those readers who are acquainted with one or both of the two most important earlier transcription systems, Yale and Wade, a comparative table has been provided on pages xvii and xviii.

Though complete in itself and suitable for home as well as classroom study, this book will be most valuable if used along with the

---

*Despite the title, it is a grammar, not a reader. The original publication is in two volumes and contains 72 lessons and several appendixes.

†The publisher is grateful to Miss Nancy Duke Lay for checking these translations and making helpful suggestions.

record set of the same name, being published concurrently. The records are based on the book, and contain (in Chinese only) the Exercises of Lessons 1 through 8 (which include every possible sound and syllable of modern spoken Mandarin), the New Words and Simple Sentences of Lessons 9 through 12, and the New Words and Texts of Lessons 13 through 30.* The corresponding record sides and bands are indicated in all these places in this book.

*The original record set, entitled *Records in Spoken Chinese*, manufactured by the China Record Company, distributed by Guozi Shudian (China Publications Centre), Peking, consists of eight ten-inch 33⅓-rpm discs, covering all 72 lessons of the original grammar book. The Dover set consists of three twelve-inch discs, covering the first thirty lessons, the pronunciation exercises of Lessons 1 through 4 being abridged to match the new text.

CONTENTS

INTRODUCTION

The Chinese language (or the Han language) is the chief language of China, and also one of the most popular and developed languages in the world.

China is a country of many nationalities, and has a population of six hundred million, about 94% of which are of the Han nationality. Each of the national minorities has its own language. The Chinese language is the language of the Han nationality, and also the common social language used among all the nationalities.

The Chinese language, according to present data, consists of eight principal dialects: the Northern dialect, the Kiangsu-Chekiang dialect, the Hunan dialect, the Kiangsi dialect, the Hakka dialect, the northern Fukien dialect, the southern Fukien dialect and the Kwangtung dialect. Above 70% of the population who use the Chinese language speak the Northern dialect. The Northern dialect district includes, in fact, the wide area north of the Yangtze River, the tract of land to the south of the Yangtze River, the west of Chenkiang and the east of Kiukiang, the four provinces of Hupeh (excepting the south-east corner), Szechwan, Yunnan and Kweichow, and last of all, the north-western part of the Hunan province. It is seldom found in the world that so many people of so wide a region speak one and the same dialect. The grammar of all the dialects is fundamentally the same, the majority of words are the same, and only the pronunciation is rather different, but in spite of that, there exist among the various dialects some corresponding phonetic relations. The present condition of the spoken Han language may be described as follows: though the various dialects are still in use, the Chinese people are taking measures to spread the popular language with the Peking speech sounds as the standard so as to unify gradually the various dialects and form a common national language.

The "ancient literary language" (文言) of the Han nation-

ality, which was once universally used in China for so long a
period, must have become established on the basis of the spoken language, but it gradually deviated more and more from
the spoken language. Hence, there appeared later a new type
of written language, which directly recorded living speech, and
kept close to the spoken language all the time. This is what we
now call the "colloquial language" (白話), which is the source
of our present national language in writing. All the works
written in the "colloquial language" are, generally speaking, based upon the Northern dialect. At the same time, a
branch of the Northern dialect, which represented the local speech
of Peking, gradually become the means of social intercourse
in the various dialect districts, and was called the "Mandarin
language" (官話). The May 4th movement in 1919 stood for writing in the colloquial language and against writing in the ancient
literary language, and destroyed the authoritative position of the
ancient literary language. As a result, the common language
of the Han nationality became gradually unified in its written
and spoken forms. The term "popular language" (普通話) was
adopted instead of the "Mandarin language". Since the found-
ing of the People's Republic of China in 1949, the written
language has become closer to the "colloquial language", and a
fundamental union of the written and spoken languages is thus
brought about; while the spoken language is further developed.

Because of various historical reasons, the Chinese language
did not reach a total unification till now. But a basis has been
established for the unification of the Chinese language, that is,
the formation of a popular language, based upon the Peking
speech sounds as the standard sounds, the Northern dialect as
the basic dialect and modern classic works written in the colloquial language as grammatical models. The modern Chinese,
which we purpose to teach, is just such a standard language.

Here are some of the chief characteristics of modern
Chinese with respect to speech sounds, grammar, words and
characters:

Speech sounds (1) The predomination of vowels. Every
character, used in the Chinese language, is a syllable by itself.
The syllable may consist of a single vowel, a compound vowel
or a vowel preceded or followed by a consonant; but a single
consonant can never form a syllable by itself, and so it cannot
represent any Chinese character. e. g.

hàn (I) yǔ (2) kě (3) ài (4)

(The Chinese language is very charming.)

These four syllables (four characters) are formed respectively by a single vowel (2), a compound vowel (4), a vowel preceded by a consonant (3) and a vowel between two consonants (1).

(2) Tones. Every syllable representing a character, has its definite tone, e. g. "mǎi" (to buy) is pronounced in a falling and rising tone, and "mài" (to sell) in a completely falling tone. The difference in tone makes for the difference in meaning, though both have the same sound elements.

(3) Aspiration and non-aspiration. Whether the beginning consonant of a syllable is aspirated or unaspirated is quite essential for ascertaining the meaning represented by the syllable, e. g. the different meanings of "bǎo" (to have eaten enough) and "pǎo" (to run) are determined by the aspiration and non-aspiration of the beginning consonant of each syllable.

Grammar and words (1) Uniformity of syntax. The word order in Chinese is very important. For example, 我帮助你 (I help you) and 你帮助我 (you help me) are opposite in meaning. 他念書 (he reads a book) cannot be changed into 書念他. 一朵香花兒 (one fragrant flower) is a word group, while 这朵花兒很香 (this flower is very fragrant) is a sentence. A modifier is usually put before that which is modified, e. g. 白馬 (a white horse), in which 白 is an adjective modifier and 馬 the central word or the word modified, and 慢慢兒地走 (walk slowly), in which 慢慢兒地 is an adverbial modifier and 走 the central word.

(2) Particles. Particles are considered a kind of weak or form word in the Chinese language. No particle possesses any concrete meaning. It cannot be used as any sentence element, and therefore cannot form any sentence by itself. Particles are used chiefly for expressing grammatical relations: they may help words in forming grammatical constructions (such as structural particles) and may express sentence moods (such as modal particles) when they are used after words and sentences.

(3) Characters and words. In Chinese, a syllable is a character in writing. There are monosyllabic words and polysyllabic words in Chinese. A monosyllabic word is represented by a character, e. g.

人 rén (man),
来 lái (to come),
好 hǎo (good).

But there are exceptions, e. g. 花兒 (flower) consisting of two characters are pronounced as one syllable (huār). Most of the polysyllabic words are dissyllabic ones, each of which is represented by two characters, e. g.

人民 rénmín (people)

幸福 xìngfú (happiness)

我們 wǒmén (we, us)

Besides, there are also words of three syllables and four syllables.

(4) Simple and compound words. From what has been said above, it is clear that a word may be represented by one character, two characters or more than two; but not every character can form a word. 1. There are characters which can each form a word, e. g. 人 (man). 2. There are characters which may each express a bit of meaning, but cannot stand alone as a word, and can only be a part of a word, e. g. 語 and 言; but these two characters can be combined into a word with a definite meaning: 語言 (language). 3. One character, which can be a word by itself, may, in combination with another character, form another word, and the second character sometimes may form a word by itself, such as 鉄路 (railway), or it may not, such as 人民 (people). 4. There are some characters which only appear in one word, such as 葡萄 (grapes), for neither 葡 nor 萄 can express any meaning by itself, and therefore cannot form another word with any other character. The words given under 1 and 4 are simple words, and those under 2 and 3 are compound words. There are various formations of compound words, and the few instances given here are used only as illustrations. For the sake of clearness, the contents of the above four points may be summed up in the following table:

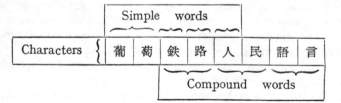

Chinese characters: The writing symbols of the Chinese language, the characters, have a history of more than three thousand years, according to excavated evidence. Notwithstanding the fact that the Chinese characters originated from a kind of hieroglyphs, they have already advanced far ahead of the stage of hieroglyphs, e. g. from these two ancient characters 〉 (the side view of a man) and 🐘 (the side view of an elephant), we can see what they symbolize, but this pictorial form is lost in the same two characters in modern writing, 人 and

象. Most of the Chinese characters indicate shape and sound, that is, one part of each character represents the sense and the other part the sound, e. g.

油 yóu (oil)　　氵 (meaning water, representing the sense)

　　　　　　　由 ("yóu" representing the sound)

桐 tóng (tree of tung oil)

　　　　　　　木 (meaning wood, representing the sense)

　　　　　　　同 ("tóng" representing the sound)

But owing to the change of character writing and speech sounds, the sound part of a great number of characters has almost lost its function and no longer represents the sound and tone of the character, e. g.

1.	江 jiāng	(river):	工	gōng
2.	鴿 gē	(dove):	合	hé
3.	筒 tǒng	(tube):	同	tóng
4.	念 niàn	(to read):	今	jīn
5.	圈 quān	(circle):	卷	juàn
6.	問 wèn	(to ask):	門	mén

For the convenience of discriminating and writing characters, they may be divided into two kinds according to their structure. Characters of the first kind are basic characters, each of which consists of a simple unit, that cannot be analyzed, e. g. 人 (man) and 水 (water). Those of the second kind are mixed characters, each of which is composed of two or more than two simple units. The characters of shape and sound belong to this kind. Comparatively speaking, a mixed character seems somewhat complicated, but it is not really difficult as soon as one makes out each component part of the character.

The number of characters is very great (the Kan-hsi Dictionary records 47,021 characters, not counting the alternative forms), but actually those in common use are only about five or six thousand. According to recent statistics, any one who knows 1,556 characters, is actually in command of 95% of the characters in general use.

The Chinese characters have played a brilliant and important role in the long history of Chinese culture. All the splendid ancient classical literature of China is preserved in these characters. In the period of the Chinese socialist construction, the Chinese characters are now used by the masses throughout the country. In the far future, they will continue to exist, and will be studied by many people. But in order to facilitate the popularization of culture and education, the characters are undergoing a reform. In January, 1956, the State Council of the

People's Republic of China promulgated the Plan of the Simplification of Characters. It aims at simplifying the characters composed of too many strokes, and at selecting one form of a character when there are two or more than two forms.

On the 11th of February, 1958, the 5th session of the 1st National People's Congress approved the Phonetic Scheme for Annotating Chinese Characters. This scheme chiefly serves to annotate the pronunciation of Chinese characters alphabetically, to facilitate the teaching of them, to unify the speech sounds and to popularize the common language. Foreigners will find it very convenient to learn the Chinese language and characters with the help of the phonetic alphabet. Teachers and research students of the Chinese language may also consider further possible reforms of the Chinese characters on the basis of the phonetic alphabet.

COMPARATIVE TABLE OF TRANSCRIPTIONS
OF CHINESE SOUNDS

Peking (this book)	Yale	Wade
a	a	a
ai	ai	ai
ao	au	ao
b	b	p
c	ts	ts', tz'
ch	ch	ch'
d	d	t
e	e, ee	e, ê, eh
ei	ei	ei
er	er	êrh
f	f	f
g	g	k
h	h	h
i, yi	i, r, y, yi, z	i, ih, ŭ
ia, ya	ya	ia, ya
iao, yao	yau	iao, yao
ie, ye	ye	ie, ieh, ye
iou, iu, you	you	iu, yu
j	j	ch
k	k	k'
l	l	l
m	m	m
n	n	n
ng	ng	ng
o	o	o
ong	ung	ung
ou	ou	ou
p	p	p'

Peking (this book)	Yale	Wade
q	ch	ch'
r	r	j
s	s	s, ss
sh	sh	sh
t	t	t'
u	u	u
ü	yu, yw	ü
ua, wa	wa	ua, wa
uai, wai	wai	uai, wai
ue	we	wê
üe, yue	ywe	üe, üeh
uei, ui, wei	wei	uei, ui, wei
uo, wo	wo	uo, wo, o
x	sy	hs
z	dz	ts, tz
zh	j	ch

Modern Chinese

Phonetics
Lesson 1

1.1 Vowels: "a", "o", "e", "i", "u", "ü"

The standard speech sounds of modern Chinese are based upon the speech sounds of Peking dialect. There are six basic vowels in Peking dialect: "a", "o", "e", "i", "u", "ü". Here is the pronunciation of these six vowels:

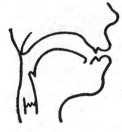

"a": It is produced by lowering the tongue, with the mouth and lips wide-open. The breath comes out freely.

"o": It is produced by keeping the tongue in a half raised position with the back of the tongue towards the soft palate, the mouth a little open and the lips slightly rounded.

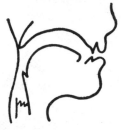

"e": It is produced by raising the back of the tongue towards the soft palate, with the mouth half open and the tongue a little lower than in the case of "o". "e" is the unrounded vowel corresponding to the rounded vowel "o".

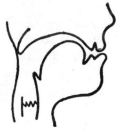

"i": It is produced by raising the front blade of the tongue towards the hard palate, with the mouth a little open and the lips flat, and then letting the breath come out between the hard palate and the blade of the tongue.

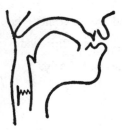

"u": It is produced by raising the back of the tongue towards the soft palate, and rounding the lips, with the mouth a little open, and then letting the breath come out between the soft palate and the back of the tongue.

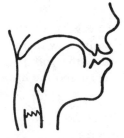

"ü": The position of the tongue is like that of "i", but the shape of the lips is different; the shape of the lips is like that of "u", but the position of the tongue is different; the mouth is kept open as little as in pronouncing "i" and "u". "ü" is the rounded vowel corresponding to the un-rounded vowel "i", and hence "ü" is produced only by keeping the tongue in the same position as in pronouncing "i" and the lips as rounded as in pronouncing "u".

1.2 Consonants: "b", "d", "g"

There are 24 consonants (including two semi-vowels "y" and "w") in Peking dialect. So far as their different positions and manners of pronunciation are concerned, they can be classified into several groups. In this lesson, only "b", "d" and "g" are introduced. These three consonants are unaspirated, voiceless, plosive sounds, because in pronouncing these consonants the passage of the breath is obstructed, and the pent-up air comes out with a pop. According to their positions of pronounciation, "b" is a labial plosive, "d" an alveolar plosive and "g" a velar plosive.

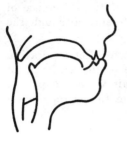

"b": It is produced by pressing the lips together, keeping the breath in the mouth for a moment, and then opening the mouth and letting the pent-up air come out. Don't send forth too much air. The vocal cords do not vibrate.

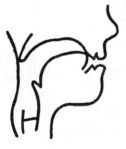

"d": It is produced by raising the tip of the tongue against the gum of the upper teeth and then drawing it away to release the pent up air with a pop. Don't send forth too much air. The vocal cords do not vibrate.

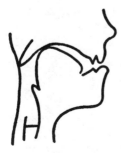

"g": It is produced by raising the back of the tongue against the soft palate, and then drawing it away to release the pent-up air with a pop. Don't send forth too much air. The vocal cords do not vibrate.

1.3 Spelling

Spelling is the joining of two or more sounds into one syllable. e. g.

$$b + a \longrightarrow ba$$
$$g + u \longrightarrow gu$$
$$d + i \longrightarrow di$$

1.4 Tones (1)

The tone is the variation of pitch (chiefly that of its height, rising and falling). The tone rises and falls by gliding and not by bounding. Every syllable in Chinese has its definite tone, and, therefore, tones are as important as vowels and consonants in forming syllables. It is only because of the difference of tones that the meanings of words are different, although the spelling is the same.

There are four tones in Peking dialect. Let us draw a short vertical line to represent the range of the variation of pitch and divide it into four equal intervals with five points. These five points, counted from the bottom to the top, represent the five degrees:

5   the high-pitch

4   the mid-high pitch

3   the middle-pitch

2   the mid-low-pitch

1   the low-pitch

The four tones in Peking dialect are represented by (1), (2), (3) and (4) in the following fig. :

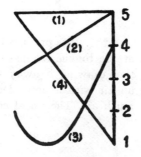

We use the pitch-graphs "⌐, ⌐, ⌐, ⌐ "to represent the four tones. But they can be simplified as follows: —, ／, ✓, ＼. They must be placed on the vowel (if there is only one vowel) or on the main vowel of a syllable.

In this lesson we only deal with the 1st and 2nd tones.

The 1st tone (55)* is a "high-level" tone. In writing it is represented by the pitch-graph "—" e. g. "gū", "bā".

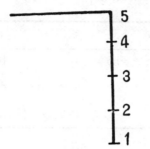

The 2nd tone (35)† is a "high-rising" tone. It is represented by the pitch-graph " ／ ". e· g. "dá", "gé".

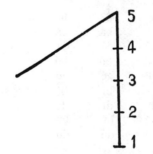

Exercises
SIDE ONE, BAND ONE

1) Read the following vowels: (to be read across)

a	o	e		a	o	e
a	a	o	o		e	e
i	u	ü		i	u	ü
i	i	u	u	ü	ü
a	o	e		i	u	ü

* That is, from 5 to 5 on the figure (remaining at level 5).
† That is, from level 3 to level 5 of the figure.

2) Read the following syllables, paying attention to the pronunciation of the consonants: (to be read across)

bo	de	bo	de
ge	bo	ge	bo
de	ge	de	ge

3) Practise the following spellings:(on the record, the columns are read first down, then across)

	a	o	e	i	u	ü
b	ba	bo	—	bi	bu	—
d	da	—	de	di	du	—
g	ga	—	ge	—	gu	—

4) Practise the following spellings and tones: (read across)

ā	ā	á	á
ǖ	ǖ	ǘ	ǘ
bā	bā	bá	bá
dā	dā	dá	dá
bō	bō	bó	bó
gē	gē	gé	gé
bī	bī	bí	bí
dī	dī	dí	dí
bū	bū	bú	bú
dū	dū	dú	dú

Home Work

1) Learn the above exercises by heart and pay special attention to the pronunciation of "o", "e" and "ü".

2) Learn the 1st tone and the 2nd tone by heart, and pay special attention to the pitch of the 2nd tone.

3) Read the vowels and consonants in this lesson as many times as you can, until you are able to write them out from your memory.

4) Write the phonetic symbols in this lesson five times.

Lesson 2

2.1 Consonants: "p", "t", "k", "m", "n", "ng"

(1) "p", "t", "k"

These three consonants are aspirated, corresponding to the unaspirated "b", "d", and "g", and so in pronouncing these consonants, the breath has to be puffed out strongly. The positions of pronunciation of these consonants are the same as those of "b", "d", and "g": "p" is a labial plosive, "t" an alveolar plosive and "k" a velar plosive.

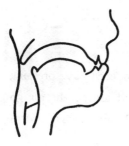

"p": When the breath is about to puff out through the lips, emit as much air as possible. The vocal cords do not vibrate.

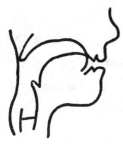

"t": When the breath is about to puff out through the mouth, emit as much air as possible. The vocal cords do not vibrate.

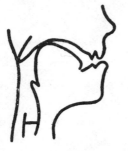

"k": When the breath is about to puff out through the mouth, emit as much air as possible. The vocal cords do not vibrate.

(2) "m", "n", "ng"

These 3 consonants are nasal, voiced sounds. The obstruction formed in the mouth in uttering "m" is like that in uttering "b", the obstruction formed in uttering "n" is like that in uttering "d", and the obstruction formed in uttering "ng" is like that in uttering "g".   The difference is that in uttering "m", "n", and "ng" the soft palate must be lowered, thus opening the nasal passage and letting the breath come out from there.   According to the positions of pronunciation, "m" is labial, "n" alveolar, and "ng" velar.

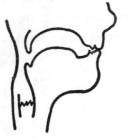

"m": It is produced by pressing the lips together, and letting the air go out through the nasal cavity. The vocal cords vibrate.

"n": It is produced by raising the tip of the tongue against the gum of the upper teeth, and letting the air come out of the nasal cavity. The vocal cords vibrate.

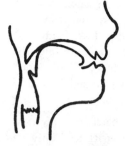

"ng": It is produced by raising the back of the tongue against the soft palate, and letting the air go out through the nasal cavity. The vocal cords vibrate. (Note: "ng" is only used at the end of a syllable.)

2.2 Compound Vowels (diphthongs and triphthongs)

A compound vowel is formed by a combination of two or three vowels. The pronunciation of a compound vowel is starting from one vowel and then moving to or towards another vowel; hence there must be changes in the position of the tongue, the opening of the mouth and the shape of the lips. There are 13 compound vowels:

```
       a   o   e   ai  ei   ao ou
  i   ia      ie           iao iou
  u   ua  uo      uai uei
  ü           üe
```

2.3 Vowels Plus Nasal Consonants

The following 16 compound sounds are spelt by putting nasal consonants after vowels:

an	en	ang	eng	ong
ian	in	iang	ing	iong
uan	uen	uang	ueng	
üan	ün			

The sound values of single vowels and compound vowels deserve special attention. A brief explanation will be given below:

1. "a" and "a" in "ia", "ua" are [A]. "a" in "ai", "uai", "an", "uan" and "üan" is the front-low vowel [a] with the lips unrounded. Strictly speaking, "a" in "ai" and "üan" is similar to [æ], while [i] should be [ɪ]. "a" in "ao", "iao", "ang", "iang", and "uang" is the back-low unrounded vowel [ɑ], and "a" in "ian" is the front mid-low, unrounded vowel [ɛ].

2. "o" or "o" in "uo", "ou" and "iou" is the back-midhigh vowel [o], but a little wider, with the lips not too rounded. The rounding of the lips becomes increasingly less from "o" to "uo", and "ou . [u] in "ou" is a little wider, while the sound of [o] in "iou" is rather weak. [o] in "ao", "iao", "ong" and "iong" is the back-high vowel [ɑ] with rounded lips and wider than [u].

3. "e" is the vowel [ɤʌ] uttered from back mid-high to mid-low with the lips unrounded; it may be written simply as [ɤ]. "e" in "ie", "üe" is the front mid-low vowel [ɛ] with the lips unrounded, while ê alone is also [ɛ]. "e" in "ei", "uei" is the front mid-high vowel [e] with the lips unrounded and [i] is a little wider, while the sound of [e] in "uei" is rather weak. "e" in "en" and "uen" is the high neutral vowel [ə], while the sound of [e] in "uen" is rather weak. "e" in "eng", "ueng" is the back mid-low vowel [ʌ] with the lips unrounded.

4. In ün, ü [y] is followed by a weak [ı] sound.

2.4 Tones (2)

In this lesson we discuss the 3rd and the 4th tones in Peking dialect.

The 3rd tone (214)* is a "falling-and-rising" tone, it descends from the mid-low pitch to the low pitch and then rises up to the mid-high pitch. It is represented by the pitch-graph "✔", e. g. "bǎ" and "nǚ".

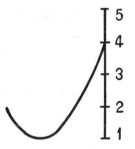

The 4th tone (51)† is a "falling" tone, it falls from high to low. The pitch-graph is " ＼ ", e. g. "tù" and "pò".

---

* That is, from level 2 through level 1 to level 4 on the figure.

† That is, from level 5 to level 1 on the figure.

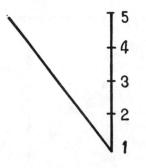

In learning the four tones the following points have to be noticed:

(1) The above figures only indicate the pitch variation of the four tones in Peking dialect. Actually the pitch of human voice is not the same for all persons.

(2) The tone represents the pitch variation, it has no relation to the intensity of sound.

(3) The four tones are different in length, and in analysis, the 3rd tone is the longest, and the 1st and the 2nd tones are longer than the 4th tone.

Exercises

SIDE ONE, BAND TWO

1) Read the following syllables, paying attention to the pronunciation of the consonants: (to be read across)

po	te	po	te		
ke	po	ke	po		
te	ke	te	ke		
bo	bo	po	po		
de	de	te	te		
ge	ge	ke	ke		
bo	de	ge	po	te	ke
mo	mo	ne	ne		
mo	ne	mo	ne		

2) Read the following compound vowels: (to be read across)

a	i	ai	a	i	ai
a	o	ao	a	o	ao
o	u	ou	o	u	ou
e	i	ei	e	i	ei
i	a	ia	i	a	ia
i	ê	ie	i	ê	ie
i	ao	iao	i	ao	iao
i	ou	iou	i	ou	iou
u	a	ua	u	a	ua
u	o	uo	u	o	uo
u	ei	uei	u	ei	uei
u	ai	uai	u	ai	uai
ü	ê	üe	ü	ê	üe

3) Read the following compound syllables and pay attention to the difference between -n and -ng: (to be read across)

an	an	ang	ang
en	en	eng	eng
an	en	ang	eng
in	in	ing	ing
uen	uen	ueng	ueng
uen	uen	ong	ong
in	uen	ing	ueng
ün	ün	iong	iong
uen	ün	ueng	iong

an	ang	ong
ian	iang	iong
uan	uang	
üan		

4) Practise the following tones: (to be read across)

ǔ	ǔ	ù	ù	ǔ	ù
bǎ	bǎ	bà	bà	bǎ	bà
pǎo	pǎo	pào	pào	pǎo	pào
kǎn	kǎn	kàn	kàn	kǎn	kàn
bǎng	bǎng	bàng	bàng	bǎng	bàng

děng	děng	dèng	dèng	děng	dèng
pìn	pǐn	pín	pīn	pǐn	pìn

ī	í	ǐ	ì
ū	ú	ǔ	ù
mō	mó	mǒ	mò
ǖn	ǘn	ǚn	ǜn
īng	íng	ǐng	ìng

Home Work

1) Learn the above exercises and pay special attention to: 1. the different pronunciation between "b" and "p", "d" and "t", "g" and "k". 2. the pronunciation of "an, en", "ang, eng", "in, uen, ün" and "ong, ing, ueng, iong". 3. the difference between the 2nd and the 3rd tones.

2) Learn all the phonetic symbols in this lesson by heart, until you can write them out from your memory.

3) Write the new phonetic symbols five times.

Lesson 3

3.1 Consonants: "f", "h", "l", "z", "c", "s"

    (1) "f" and "h"

These two consonants are voiceless fricatives. In pronouncing them, the passage of the breath is small but not completely obstructed, so that the breath comes out with friction. According to their positions of pronunciation, "f" is a labio-dental fricative, and "h" a velar fricative.

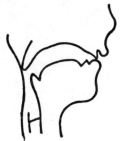

    "f"; Press the lower-lip against the upper teeth, and let the breath come out with friction. The vocal cords do not vibrate.

    "h": Raise the back of the tongue towards the soft palate, and let the breath rub through the channel thus made. The vocal cords do not vibrate.

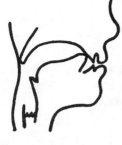

(2) "l"

It is a voiced alveolar lateral. It is produced by raising the tip of the tongue against the gum of the upper teeth to stop the air passage, and thus letting the air come out by the sides of the tongue. The vocal cords vibrate.

(3) "z" and "c"

"z" is an unaspirated voiceless affricate, and "c" is an aspirated voiceless affricate. In pronouncing them, the air passage is completely obstructed, then the tip of the tongue moves away a little and the air is let out by rubbing through the narrow channel in the mouth, and so the obstruction and the friction come close together. Both of them are blade-alveolar affricates.

"z": Press the tip of the tongue against the gum of the upper teeth, and let the breath puff out and rub through the narrow channel thus made between the tip of the tongue and the teeth. Don't emit too much air. The vocal cords do not vibrate. "c": The pronunciation of this sound is the same as that of "z" sound. The only difference is that "c" is pronounced with a strong puff of breath.

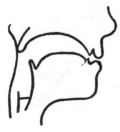

(4) "s"

It is a blade-alveolar voiceless fricative, and is produced by lowering the tip of the tongue to the back of the lower teeth, and letting the breath rub through the narrow channel between the middle of the blade and the upper teeth.

3.2 The Blade-alveolar Vowel after "z", "c", "s"

The blade-alveolar vowel [ʅ] after "z", "c", "s" is also represented by "i". There cannot be any confusion, because the vowel sound of "i" [i] never occurs after "z" "c", "s" in Peking dialect. This vowel [ʅ] only occurs after z, c, s, therefore it sounds like the voiced prolongation and weakening of the fricative element of the preceding consonant.

3.3 Retroflex Vowel "er (-r)"

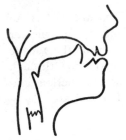

This sound is produced with the tongue a little forward from the position of the mixed vowel "e" (the international phonetic symbol is [ə]), with the tip of the tongue turned up towards the hard palate, thus producing "e" sound with a curved tongue "r". In pronouncing this sound, keep the mouth from a little open at first to a little close.

3.4 Components of Chinese Characters (1)

The Chinese characters, the written symbols of the Chinese language, are, in general, constituted of several parts. Each part of a Chinese character is called a "component of the Chinese character" (some components are also characters when they stand by themselves). The components of Chinese characters are composed of a number of basic strokes. Therefore, we should pay much attention to the ways of writing of these basic strokes and the order of the strokes in making any component (or character).

In this lesson, we only deal with the basic strokes of Chinese characters. The following seven basic strokes are the most elementary:

Exercises

SIDE ONE, BAND THREE

1) Read the following syllables, paying attention to the pronunciation of the consonants:

fo	fo	he	he	le	le
fo	fo	he	he	le	le

zi	zi	ci	ci
si	si	zi	zi

zi	ci	si	zi	ci	si
si	ci	zi	si	ci	zi

2) Read the following spellings: (to be read across)

fu	fú	fŭ	fù
hāo	háo	hǎo	hào
luō	luó	luǒ	luò
zāo	záo	zǎo	zào
zān	zán	zǎn	zàn
cāi	cái	cǎi	cài
sōng	sóng	sǒng	sòng
cī	cí	cǐ	cì

3) Read the following retroflex vowel "er":
    (to be read across)

er	er	er					
ēr	ér	ěr	èr				
ēr	ēr	ér	ér	ěr	ěr	èr	èr

4) Practise writing the basic strokes.

Home Work

1) Read the first three sections of the exercises several times and pay attention to the pronunciation of "z" and "c".

2) Copy the basic strokes of Chinese characters in this lesson several times.

3) Write the new phonetic symbols and basic strokes of characters five times.

Lesson 4

4.1 Consonants: "zh", "ch", "sh", "r", "j", "q", "x"

(1) "zh" and "ch"

"zh" is an unaspirated voiceless affricate, and "ch" is an aspirated voiceless affricate. In pronouncing them, the passage of the breath is completely obstructed, then the tip of the tongue moves away a little and the air is let through by rubbing the narrow channel in the mouth. The obstruction and the friction come close together. These two consonants are blade-palatal sounds (or retroflex sounds).

"zh": Turn up the tip of the tongue against the hard palate, and then let the breath puff out and rub through the channel between the tip of the tongue and the hard palate. Don't emit too much air. The vocal cords do not vibrate.

"ch": The pronunciation of this sound is the same as that of "zh" sound. The only difference is that "ch" is produced with a strong puff of breath.

(2) "sh" and "r"

These two consonants are also blade-palatal sounds. "sh" is a voiceless fricative and "r" is a voiced fricative.

"sh": Turn up the tip of the tongue near the hard palate, and let the air rub through the channel between the tip of the tongue and the hard palate. The vocal cords do not vibrate.

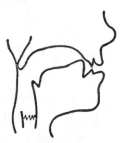

"r": It is the voiced sound corresponding to "sh", and so in producing this sound the vocal cords vibrate. (The blade-palatal vowel [ʐ] after "zh", "ch", "sh", "r" is also represented by "i". There can be no confusion, because the vowel sound of "i" [i] never occurs after "zh", "ch", "sh", "r" in Peking dialect. This vowel [ʐ] only occurs after "zh", "ch", "sh", "r", therefore it sounds like the voiced prolongation and weakening of the fricative element of the preceding consonant.

(3) "j" and "q"

"j" is an unaspirated voiceless affricate and "q" an aspirated voiceless affricate. In producing these two sounds, the air passage is completely obstructed, then it is slowly opened and the air is let through by rubbing the narrow channel in the mouth. The obstruction and the friction come close together. These two consonants are front-palatal sounds.

"j": Raise the front of the tongue to the hard palate, place the tip of the tongue against the back of the lower teeth, and then let the air puff out and rub through the channel between the front of the tongue and the hard palate. Don't emit too much air. The vocal cords do not vibrate.

"ㄑ": The pronunciation of this sound is the same as that of "j" sound, except that it should be produced with a strong puff of breath.

(4) "x"

"x" is a voiceless fricative. It is produced by raising the front of the tongue near the hard palate, and then letting the air rub through the channel between the front of the tongue and the hard palate. The vocal cords do not vibrate.

4.2 The Syllabic Construction of Peking Dialect

(1) In Peking dialect, a single vowel, a compound vowel or a vowel with a consonant (whether the consonant stands before the vowel or after) may form a syllable, but a consonant cannot form a syllable by itself. Every syllable has its definite tone. e. g.

è	(餓 hungry)		ài	(愛 to love)
ēn	(恩 favour)		hé	(河 river)
bǎo	(飽 full, to eat one's fill)		shuāng	(霜 frost)

(2) Every syllable is a Chinese character. Therefore, according to the Chinese traditional method of phonetic analysis, the sound of a character may be generally divided into "shēng" 声母 (the consonant at the beginning of a syllable) and "yùn" 韻母 (the rest of the syllable after the consonant). Besides, every character has its proper tone. In "hé" and "shuāng" given in the above examples, "h" and "sh" are "shēng's" 声母, "e" and "uang" are "yùn's" 韻母; "hé" is in the second tone, and "shuāng" is in the first tone. But there are also characters which are composed of only "yùn" 韻母, such as: "ēn" in the above examples.

(3) Every syllable in Peking Dialect consists of a "shēng" and a "yùn". A "yùn" can be a single (main) vowel, e.g. chá (tea); it can also be a vowel plus a medial vowel and a "yùn ending", e. g. biǎo (watch); sometimes it can be a medial-vowel and a main vowel. e. g. shuō (to speak, to say);

or only a vowel and a "yùn ending", e.g. kàn (to see). There are only three medial vowels: "i", "u" and "ü". "yùn's" can be divided into four types: 1. those without medial vowel or without "i", "u", "ü" as the main vowel; 2. those with the medial vowel "i" or using "i" as the main vowel; 3. those with the medial vowel "u" or using "u" as the main vowel; 4. those with the medial vowel "ü" or using "ü" as the main vowel. Any vowel can be a main vowel and any consonant (except "-ng") can be a "shēng". The combinations of "shēng" and "yùn" are chiefly determined by the positions of articulation of "shēng" and the type of "yùn". The following table shows all the possible combinations of "shēng" and "yùn":

声母 韻母类别 types of yùn shēng	1	2	3	4
b p m	+	+	+	−
f	+	−	+	−
d t	+	+	+	−
n l	+	+	+	+
z c s	+	−	+	−
zh ch sh r	+	−	+	−
j q x	−	+	−	+
g k h	+	−	+	−
0	+	+	+	+

    " + " indicates that "shēng" can go with "yùn", while " − " indicates that it cannot.
    "0" indicates zero "shēng".

4.3 Four Points about the Ways of Writing
    (1) When "i", "u", "ü" and a "yùn" 韻母 beginning with "i", "u" or "ü" are not preceded by any "shēng" 声母, they

must be written as follows:

yi, ya, ye, yan, you, yao, yin,

yang, ying, yong.

wu, wa, wo, wai, wei,

wan, wen, wang, weng.

yu, yue, yuan, yun.

(The two dots on ü are omitted.)

(2) When "ü" or a "yùn" 韻母 beginning with "ü" spells with "j", "q", "x", they may be written as "ju", "qu", "xu", without the two dots on "ü", but when the consonants "n", "l" are followed by "ü", the two dots cannot be omitted, e.g. "nü", "lü".

(3) "iou", "uei" and "uen" are basic forms, but they must be written as "—iu", "—ui" and "—un", when they are preceded by a consonant. The tone-graph is placed on the last vowel "u" or "i" in the simplified forms "—iu" and "—ui", e. g. "niú", "guì".

(4) In case two syllables of which the second one begins with "a", "o", "e" should run into each other and cause confusion in pronunciation, the dividing sign " ' " must be used. e. g.

⎰ fáng'ài 妨碍 (to hinder)
⎱ fāngài 翻盖 (to rebuild)

4.4 Components of Chinese Characters (2)

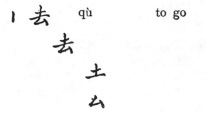

去 qù   to go

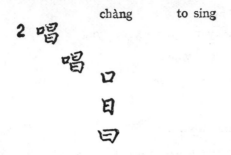

chàng   to sing

2 唱

Exercises
SIDE ONE, BAND FOUR

1) Read the following syllables, paying attention to the pronunciation of the consonants: (to be read across)

zhi	chi	shi	ri
zhi	chi	shi	ri
zhi	zhi	chi	chi
shi	shi	ri	ri

ji	qi	xi	ji	qi	xi
ji	ji	qi	qi	xi	xi
ji	qi	ji	qi	ji	qi
qi	xi	qi	xi	qi	xi

2) Read the following syllables and pay attention to their ways of writing:
   1. è, ài, ǒu, yǔ, wǎng, yǒng.
   2. yōu, wán, yá, yì, yíng, wǒ, wǔ, wèng, yūan, yǔn.
   3. jǔ, qù, xuǎn, qióng, lǚ, nǚ.
   4. huí, wèi, guì, kuí, wěi, liū, qiú, diū, jiǔ, xiù, lún, wén, chūn, shùn, tóng, wēng.
   5. ⎰ yīn'àn   陰暗   (gloomy)
      ⎱ yínán   疑难   (puzzle)
      ⎰ míngē   民歌   (folk song)
      ⎱ míng'é   名额   (number)
      ⎰ fáng'ài 妨碍   (to hinder)
      ⎱ fāngài   翻盖   (to rebuild)

3) Read the following dissyllabic words:
   1. zhuānjiā   2. qīngnián   3. sīxiǎng
   4. yīnsù   5. yánjiū   6. rénmín
   7. niúnǎi   8. zázhì   9. diàndēng
   10. wèntí   11. fùnǚ

4) Notice the basic strokes of the following components of Chinese characters and copy them several times:

1	土	一 十 土
2	厶	ㄥ 厶
3	口	丶 冂 口
4	目	丨 冂 冂 目
5	曰	丶 冂 冃 曰

Home Work

1) Learn the exercises of this lesson by heart, and pay attention to the pronunciation of "zh" "ch", "sh", "r", "j" and "q".

2) Copy the second section of the exercises, read it aloud.

3) Copy the components of Chinese characters five times.

Lesson 5
SIDE TWO

5.1 Table of the Chinese Phonetic Alphabet

(the names of the phonemes are read on the record)

letters			names	letters			names
printed form		written form		printed form		writtten form	
A	a	𝒜 𝑎	[a]	N	n	𝒩 𝑛	[nə]
B	b	ℬ 𝑏	[pə]	O	o	𝒪 𝑎	[o]
C	c	𝒞 𝑐	[ts'ə]	P	p	𝒫 𝑝	[p'ə]
D	d	𝒟 𝑑	[tə]	Q	q	𝒬 𝑞	[tɕ'iou]
E	e	ℰ 𝑒	[ɤ]	R	r	ℛ 𝑟	[ar]
F	f	ℱ 𝑓	[əf]	S	s	𝒮 𝑠	[əs]
G	g	𝒢 𝑔	[kə]	T	t	𝒯 𝑡	[t'ə]
H	h	ℋ 𝒽	[xa]	U	u	𝒰 𝑢	[u]
I	i	ℐ 𝑖	[i]	V	v	𝒱 𝑣	[və] *
J	j	𝒥 𝑗	[tɕie]	W	w	𝒲 𝑤	[wa]
K	k	𝒦 𝑘	[k'ə]	X	x	𝒳 𝑥	[ɕi]
L	l	ℒ 𝑙	[əl]	Y	y	𝒴 𝑦	[ja]
M	m	ℳ 𝑚	[əm]	Z	z	𝒵 𝑧	[tsə]

*The letter "v" is used only in spelling the words adopted from foreign languages, languages of national minorities and various dialects.

5.2 Table of the Chinese Vowels and Table of the Chinese Consonants

(1) Table of the Chinese Vowels
(on the record, read as "a o e ê i u ü er")

	tip-tongue vowels		palatal vowels		
	blade-alveolar	blade-palatal	front	central	back
high (close)	-i	-i	i ü		u
mid-high (half-close)			(e)		e o
mid-low (half-open)		er	ê	(e)	
low (open)				(a) a	(a)

The blade-alveolar vowel and the blade-palatal vowel are represented respectively by the borrowed letters from Swedish [ʅ] and [ʮ]. "er" may be represented by the international phonetic symbol [ər].

(2) Table of the Chinese Consonants
(on the record, read across, then down)

	unaspirated voiceless plosives and affricates	aspirated, voiceless plosives and affricates	voiced na- sals	voice- less frica- tives	voiced lateral, voiced fricative
labial	b [p]	p [p']	m [m]	f [f]	
alveolar	d [t]	t [t']	n [n]		l [l]
blade-alveolar	z [ts]	c [ts']		s [s]	
blade-palatal	zh [tʂ]	ch [tʂ']		sh [ʂ]	r [ʐ]
palatal	j [tɕ]	q [tɕ']		x [ɕ]	
velar	g [k]	k [k']	ng [ŋ]	h [x]	

5.3 Table of Compound Vowels and Vowels Plus Nasal Consonants
(on the record, read across, then down)

	a	o	e	ai	ei	ao	ou	an	en	ang	eng	ong
i	ia		ie			iao	iou	ian	in	iang	ing	iong
u	ua	uo		uai	uei			uan	uen	uang	ueng	
ü			üe					üan	ün			

Table of the Speech Sounds of Peking Dialect

(This table is continued on the following two pages. On the record, the columns are read downward, beginning "ba, pa, ma, ...")

聲 yùn / 母 shēng	a	o	e	-i	er	ai	ei	ao	ou	an	en	ang	eng	ong
b	ba	bo				bai	bei	bao		ban	ben	bang	beng	
p	pa	po				pai	pei	pao	pou	pan	pen	pang	peng	
m	ma	mo				mai	mei	mao	mou	man	men	mang	meng	
f	fa	fo					fei		fou	fan	fen	fang	feng	
d	da		de			dai	dei	dao	dou	dan		dang	deng	dong
t	ta		te			tai		tao	tou	tan		tang	teng	tong
n	na		ne			nai	nei	nao	nou	nan	nen	nang	neng	nong
l	la		le			lai	lei	lao	lou	lan		lang	leng	long
z	za		ze	zi		zai	zei	zao	zou	zan	zen	zang	zeng	zong
c	ca		ce	ci		cai		cao	cou	can	cen	cang	ceng	cong
s	sa		se	si		sai		sao	sou	san	sen	sang	seng	song
zh	zha		zhe	zhi		zhai	zhei	zhao	zhou	zhan	zhen	zhang	zheng	zhong
ch	cha		che	chi		chai		chao	chou	chan	chen	chang	cheng	chong
sh	sha		she	shi		shai	shei	shao	shou	shan	shen	shang	sheng	
r			re	ri				rao	rou	ran	ren	rang	reng	rong
j														
q														
x														
g	ga		ge			gai	gei	gao	gou	gan	gen	gang	geng	gong
k	ka		ke			kai		kao	kou	kan	ken	kang	keng	kong
h	ha		he			hai	hei	hao	hou	han	hen	hang	heng	hong
o	a		e		er	ai		ao	ou	an	en	ang		

yùn shēng	2								
	i	ia	iao	ie	iou	ian	in	iang	ing	iong
b	bi		biao	bie		bian	bin		bing	
p	pi		piao	pie		pian	pin		ping	
m	mi		miao	mie	miu	mian	min		ming	
f										
d	di		diao	die	diu	dian			ding	
t	ti		tiao	tie		tian			ting	
n	ni		niao	nie	niu	nian	nin	niang	ning	
l	li	lia	liao	lie	liu	lian	lin	liang	ling	
z										
c										
s										
zh										
ch										
sh										
r										
j	ji	jia	jiao	jie	jiu	jian	jin	jiang	jing	jiong
q	qi	qia	qiao	qie	qiu	qian	qin	qiang	qing	qiong
x	xi	xia	xiao	xie	xiu	xian	xin	xiang	xing	xiong
g										
k										
h										
o	yi	ya	yao	ye	you	yan	yin	yang	ying	yong

yùn\shēng	3									4			
	u	ua	uo	uai	uei	uan	un	uang	ueng	ü	üe	üan	ün
b	bu												
p	pu												
m	mu												
f	fu												
d	du		duo		dui	duan	dun						
t	tu		tuo		tui	tuan	tun						
n	nu		nuo			nuan				nü	nüe		
l	lu		luo			luan	lun			lü	lüe		
z	zu		zuo		zui	zuan	zun						
c	cu		cuo		cui	cuan	cun						
s	su		suo		sui	suan	sun						
zh	zhu	zhua	zhuo	zhuai	zhui	zhuan	zhun	zhuang					
ch	chu		chuo	chuai	chui	chuan	chun	chuang					
sh	shu	shua	shuo	shuai	shui	shuan	shun	shuang					
r	ru		ruo		rui	ruan	run						
j										ju	jue	juan	jun
q										qu	que	quan	qun
x										xu	xue	xuan	xun
g	gu	gua	guo	guai	gui	guan	gun	guang					
k	ku	kua	kuo	kuai	kui	kuan	kun	kuang					
h	hu	hua	huo	huai	hui	huan	hun	huang					
o	wu	wa	wo	wai	wei	wan	wen	wang	weng	yu	yue	yuan	yun

5.4 Components of Chinese Characters (3) —

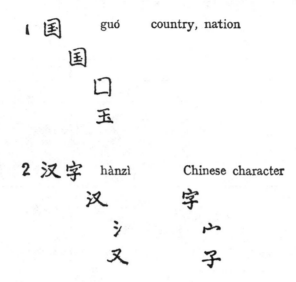

1 国   guó   country, nation

国
口
玉

2 汉字   hànzì   Chinese character

汉   字
氵   宀
又   子

Exercises

SIDE TWO

1) Read the Table of Chinese Phonetic Alphabet.

2) Practise reading the vowels and consonants:

a) Read aloud the vowels (according to the Table of the Chinese Vowels).

b) Read aloud the consonants several times according to the order of the position and manner of pronunciation as shown in the Table of the Chinese Consonants.

3) Read several times the Table of Compound Vowels and Vowels Plus Nasal Consonants.

4) Learn the Table of the Speech Sounds of Peking Dialect.

5) Pay attention to the basic strokes of the following components of Chinese characters and copy them.

1	口	丨 冂 口
2	玉	一 二 千 王 玉
3	氵	丶 冫 氵
4	又	丁 又
5	宀	丶 丶 宀
6	子	乛 了 子

Home Work

1) Review the Chinese vowels and consonants, and try to compare them with those of your own language.

2) Copy the alphabet (both the printed and the written).

3) Write the components of Chinese characters in this lesson five times.

Lesson 6

6.1 The Change of Tones

In the speech sounds of Peking dialect, the tones of syllables spoken in succession are different from those of the same syllables spoken separately. This difference is called the change of tones. The important rules of the change of tones are as follows:

(1) The neutral tone (or the light tone)

The four tones in the speech sounds of Peking dialect mentioned in the first two lessons, are the tones of stressed or accented syllables. In Chinese, when we read words separately, we always read it as a stressed syllable and therefore every word is given its own tone. In speaking, when a word is unstressed, it loses its original tone and becomes weak and short, that is to say, it becomes light in tone. For the convenience of teaching, the neutral tone is represented by the sign "o" in writing. Strictly speaking, the neutral tone is much varied in pitch. The pitch of the neutral tone of a syllable is decided by the tone of the syllable preceding it and not by its original tone. The general rules are as follows:

After the 1st tone, the neutral tone is a semi-low light tone (2nd degree). e. g.

       tādě 他的 (his)   ┐ .┤

After the 2nd tone, it is a middle light tone (3rd degree) e. g.

       shéidě 誰的 (whose)   ╱ ·┤

After the 3rd tone, it is a semi-high light tone (4th degree). e. g.

       nǐdě 你的 (your)   ↅ ·┤

After the 4th tone, it is a low light tone (1st degree). e. g.

dàdê	大的	(big one)	˥˩ ·˩

(2) A syllable of the 3rd tone followed by a syllable of the 1st, 2nd, 4th, or neutral tone is pronounced only with a falling tone without its final rising, that is, its pitch becomes 21 (˨˩).* We call this falling tone the half-third tone. e. g.

3 + 1	˨˩˦ ˥˥ ⟶ ˨˩ ˥˥	xiǎoshuō	小說 (novel)
3 + 2	˨˩˦ ˧˥ ⟶ ˨˩ ˧˥	zǔguó	祖国 (fatherland)
3 + 4	˨˩˦ ˥˩ ⟶ ˨˩ ˥˩	qǐngzuò	請坐 (Please, sit down.)
3 + 0	˨˩˦ ·˦ ⟶ ˨˩ ·˦	xǐhuân	喜欢 (like, fond of)

(3) When a third tone is followed by another third tone, then the first third tone becomes a second tone (it is still marked in the third tone in writing). e. g.

3 + 3	˨˩˦ ˨˩˦ ⟶ ˧˥ ˨˩˦	hěnlěng	很冷 (very cold)

(4) When a third tone is followed by another third tone which has become a neutral tone, the first third tone is pronounced sometimes in the second tone and sometimes in the half-third tone. e. g.

3 + 0	˨˩˦ ·˦ ⟶ ˧˥ ·˧	lǎoshû	老鼠 (rat)
3 + 0	˨˩˦ ·˦ ⟶ ˨˩ ·˦	jiějiê	姐姐 (elder sister)

(5) When a fourth tone is followed by another fourth tone, the first one does not fall so low as the 2nd one, they are pronounced as 53 51.† e. g.

4 + 4	˥˩ ˥˩ ⟶ ˥˧ ˥˩	zàijiàn	再見 (Goodbye.)

* That is, from level 2 to level 1.

† That is, the first one falls only to level 3, the second one all the way to level 1.

6.2 Components of Chinese Characters (4)

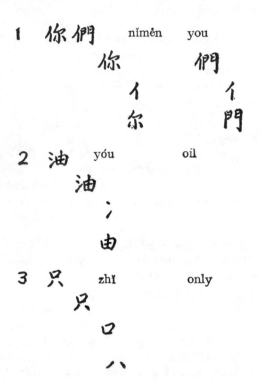

1 你們   nǐmèn   you

2 油   yóu   oil

3 只   zhǐ   only

Exercises
SIDE THREE, BAND ONE

1) Practise reading the following neutral tones:
(to be read across)

chūqů	zhūzi	māmå	bāngzhů
láile	xíngle	shénmò	péngyðu
míngzi	dǒngle	mǎibå	shàngwů
xièxiě	dìfång	wàngle	kèqi

2) Practise reading the half-third tones:
(to be read across)

Běijīng	huǒchē	hǎijūn	zhǐhuī
zǔguó	zhǔxí	jiǎnchá	xuǎnzé
zhǔyì	jiěfàng	gǎnxiè	lǐngxiù
běnzi	lízi	xǐhuån	

3) Practise reading the third tones followed by other third tones: (to be read across)

biǎoyǎn   zhǎnlǎn   shǒubiǎo
xuǎnjǔ   yǐngxiǎng

4) Practise reading the third tones followed by light tones (which are originally third tones):

xiǎngxiǎng   kěyi   nǎinǎi   yǐzi

5) Practise reading the 4th tones followed by other 4th tones: (to be read across)

shìjiè   wànsuì   sùshè
yùndòng   zhùyì   zhèngzhì

6) Distinguish the following difficult sounds (1):

(1) b, p

bǎo	飽	full, to eat one's fill
pǎo	跑	to run
bǎole	飽了	already full
pǎole	跑了	to have run away
bēi	背	to carry on one's back
pēi	披	to put over one's shoulders
bēizhe	背着	carrying on one's back
pēizhe	披着	putting over one's shoulders

(2) d, t

dìng	釘	to nail, a nail
tīng	听	to listen, to hear
wǒdìng	我釘	I nail.
wǒtīng	我听	I listen.
dǎng	擋	to cover, to stand in one's way
tǎng	躺	to lie
dǎngzhe	擋着	covering, standing in one's way
tǎngzhe	躺着	lying

(3) g, k

gàn	干	to do
kàn	看	to see, to look at
gànwán	干完	to have done, finished
kànwán	看完	to have read through

gōng	宮	palace
kōng	空	vacancy
tiāngōng	天宮	celestial palace
tiānkōng	天空	sky, heaven

(4) zh, ch

zhú	竹	bamboo
chú	厨	kitchen
zhúzǐ	竹子	bamboo
chúzǐ	厨子	cook
zhǔn	准	exact, punctual
chǔn	蠢	awkward, stupid
zhēnzhǔn	眞准	really exact, punctual
zhēnchǔn	眞蠢	really awkward

(5) j, q

jī	鷄	chicken
qī	漆	lacquer, to lacquer
yóujī	油鷄	kind of chicken
yóuqī	油漆	lacquer, resinous varnish
juàn	倦	tired
quàn	劝	to persuade, to advise
bújuàn	不倦	not tired
búquàn	不劝	not to persuade or advise

(6) q, x

qíng	晴	fine, clear
xíng	行	to walk, all right
qínglê	晴了	to have cleared up
xínglê	行了	that will do, that is right

(7) j, x

jù	剧	play
xù	序	order, preface
jùmù	剧目	program
xùmù	序幕	prelude

7) Notice the basic strokes of the components of Chinese characters in this lesson and copy them.

1	亻	丿 亻
2	尔	乀 (丿 乀)
		小 (亅 ⺌ 小)
3	門	丨 厂 厂 厂 厂 門 門 門
4	由	丶 冂 曰 由 由
5	八	丿 八

Home Work

1) Read the exercises in this lesson several times, and pay special attention to the following:

  1) The second tone followed by the light tone;

  2) The pitch of the half-third tone;

  3) The difference between the aspirated sounds and the unaspirated sounds.

2) Copy the components of Chinese characters in this lesson five times.

Lesson 7

7.1 Summary on Tones

(1) The four tones:

ā	á	ǎ	à
zhē	zhé	zhě	zhè
jū	jú	jǔ	jù
qīng	qíng	qǐng	qìng
chōng	chóng	chǒng	chòng

(2) Neutral tones (light tones):

jīntiǎn	今天	(to-day)
míngtiǎn	明天	(to-morrow)
wǎnlė	晚了	(late)
dìfǎng	地方	(place)

(3) Changes of the 3rd tone:

3 + 1	⌄¬→⌄¬	shǒudū	首都	(capital)
3 + 2	⌄ィ→⌄ィ	zhěngqí	整齐	(tidiness)
3 + 3	⌄⌄→ィ⌄	jiǎngyǎn	講演	(to give a speech)
3 + 4	⌄∨→⌄∨	lǐngxiù	領袖	(leader)
3 + 0	⌄·¹→⌄·¹	wǎnshǎng	晚上	(night)
3 + 0	⌄·¹→ィ·¹	děngděng	等等	(wait for a while)

(4) The pronunciation of two successive 4th tones:

4 + 4   ∨∨ ⟶ ⅄∨   wànsuì 万岁 (Long live...)

7.2 Tones Deserving Special Attention

(1) Light tones:

míngtiǎn	wánlė	chúzǐ
shéiyǎ	wǒmėn	dǒnglė
děngděng	kěyǐ	yǎnjǐng

shìdě   xièxiě   zhùzî
duìlě

(2) 2nd tones plus 1st tones:
     hóngjūn   guójiā   chénggōng   Nánjīng
(3) 2nd tones plus 2nd tones:
     rénmín   hépíng   wénxué   yínháng
(4) 4th tones plus 2nd tones:
     Liènìng   èwén   zhìfú   liànxí

7.3 Discrimination of Tones

Shānxī	山西	(Shansi)
Shǎnxī	陝西	(Shensi)
zhǔyì	主义	(doctrine)
zhùyì	注意	(notice)
nǔlì	努力	(endeavor, effort)
núlì	奴隶	(slave)
yànhuì	宴会	(banquet)
yānhuī	烟灰	(ashes, soot)
dǒnglě	懂了	(to have understood)
dònglě	冻了	(frozen)
zhòngshì	重视	(to attach importance to, to deem highly)
zhōngshí	忠实	(faithful, loyal)
zhīyuán	支援	(to aid, to give support to)
zhìyuàn	志愿	(voluntary)
yǎnjìng	眼晴	(eye)
yǎnjìng	眼镜	(eye-glasses)
zhèngzhí	正直	(upright, righteous)
zhēngzhí	争执	(dispute)
zhèngzhì	政治	(politics)
tōngzhī	通知	(to notify, to inform)
tóngzhì	同志	(comrade)
tǒngzhì	统治	(control)
shíyàn	实验	(experiment)
shíyán	食盐	(salt)
shìyàn	试验	(test)
shìyǎn	试演	(rehearsal)
shìyán	誓言	(oath, pledge)

7.4 Components of Chinese Characters (5)

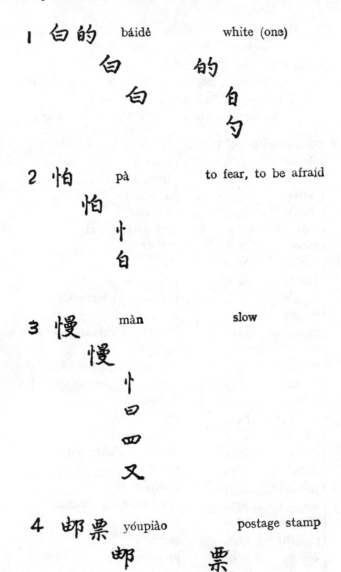

1 白的   báidê   white (one)

2 怕   pà   to fear, to be afraid

3 慢   màn   slow

4 邮票   yóupiào   postage stamp

Exercises
SIDE THREE, BAND TWO

1) Read the following four tones: (to be read across)

pāng	páng	pǎng	pàng
pīn	pín	pǐn	pìn
tān	tán	tǎn	tàn
kē	ké	kě	kè
zhōu	zhóu	zhǒu	zhòu
chēng	chéng	chěng	chèng
shē	shé	shě	shè
qiāng	qiáng	qiǎng	qiàng

Zhōngguójiěfàng
jīngshénkěpèi
shēnghuógǎishàn
fēichánggǎnxiè

2) Read the 2nd section of this lesson several times.
   (to be read across)

3) Read the 3rd section of this lesson several times (Discrimination of tones).

4) Notice the basic strokes of the components of Chinese characters in this lesson and copy them.

1	白	ノ	イ	白	白	白
2	勺	ノ	勹	勺		
3	忄	丶	忄	忄		
4	皿	丶	冂	冂	皿	皿
5	阝	㇇	阝	阝		
6	西	一	厂	冏	兩	兩 西
7	示	一	二	示	.	

Home Work

1) Read the text and exercises in this lesson as many times as you can, paying special attention to the 2nd and 3rd sections.

2) Copy the components of the Chinese characters in this lesson five times.

Lesson 8

8.1 The Retroflex Ending "-r"

In Chinese, there are many words at the end of which the vowels are pronounced with the retroflex "r" Such vowels are called retroflex vowels, for the retroflex "r" and the vowel coming before it have been combined into one syllable. Some retroflex vowels are formed by adding the retroflex "r" to the vowels, and some are formed by dropping the final vowels or consonants out of words, and then adding the retroflex "r" to the main vowels. But in writing, only "r" is put after the original syllable.

(1) With "-r" added:

(a) "-a", "-o", "-e", "-u": "-r" is added directly. e. g.

xìfǎr (xìfǎr)	戏法兒	(trick, stunt)
gēr (gēr)	歌兒	(song)
cuòr (cuòr)	錯兒	(mistake)
xiǎotùr (xiǎotùr)	小兎兒	(little rabbit)

(b) "-ai", "-ei", "-an", "-en": "-r" is added after the final vowels or consonants have been dropped. e. g.

gàir (gàr)	盖兒	(cover)
wèir (wèr)	味兒	(smell)
pángbiānr (pángbiār)	旁边兒	(edge, margin, side)
fēnr (fēr)	分兒	(mark, work-unit)

(c) "-ng": The vowel before "-ng" must be nasalized, and is pronounced with the retroflex "r" (that is, in pronunciation, the breath is let out of the mouth and the nasal cavity at the same time). Here for the convenience of writing, "ng" is used as a symbol representing the nasalized element. e. g.

dànhuángr (dànhuángr)	蛋黃兒	(the yolk of an egg)
bǎndèngr (bǎndèngr)	板凳兒	(stool)

(2) With "er" added:

(a) "-i", "-ü": "er" is added after "-i" "-ü". e. g.

  xiǎojīr (xiǎojiēr)　　小鷄兒　(chicken)

  xiǎoyúr (xiǎoyuér)　　小魚兒　(little fish)

(b) "-in": "er" is added after the final consonant has been dropped. e. g.

  xìnr (xièr)　　　　信兒　　(message)

(c) "-i": "i" after "zh", "ch", "sh", "r", "z", "c", "s" is changed into "er". e. g.

  shìr (shèr)　　　　事兒　　(matter, business)

8.2 Polysyllables

(1) Dissyllables:

fēijī	飞机	(aeroplane)
Sūlián	苏联	(The Soviet Union)
yīngyǒng	**英勇**	**(valiant)**
yīyuàn	医院	(hospital)
nóngcūn	农村	(village)
wénxué	文学	(literature)
niúnǎi	牛奶	(milk)
shídài	时代	(times)
Běijīng	北京	(Peking)
zhǔxí	主席	(chairman)
zǒngtǒng	总統	(president)
jiěfàng	解放	(liberation)
yònggōng	用功	(studious)
dàxué	大学	(university)
zhèngfǔ	政府	(government)
jìhuà	計划	(plan)

(2) Trisyllables:

gòngqīngtuán	共青团	(The Communist Youth League)
hézuòshè	合作社	(co-operative store)
bówùyuàn	博物院	(museum)

(3) Four syllables:

chíjiǔhépíng	持久和平	(lasting peace)
guānliáozhǔyì	官僚主义	(bureaucracy)
xīnwénjìzhě	新聞記者	(journalist)

8.3 Components of Chinese Characters (6)

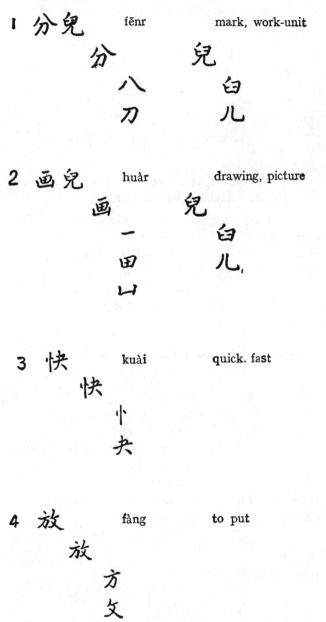

1 分兒　　fēnr　　　　mark, work-unit

分　　　　兒
八　　　　白
刀　　　　儿

2 画兒　　huàr　　　　drawing, picture

画　　　　兒
一　　　　白
田　　　　儿
凵

3 快　　　kuài　　　　quick. fast

快
忄
夬

4 放　　　fàng　　　　to put

放
方
攵

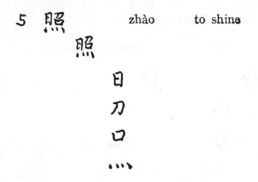

5 照   zhào   to shine

Exercises
SIDE THREE, BAND THREE

1) Practise the following retroflex vowels: (to be read down)

wánr   yíkuàir
biānr   gāngbǐtóur
zhèr   liànxíběnr
nàr   { hǎohāordė
mòshuǐr   { mànmānrdė
shíhòur

2) Distinguish the following difficult sounds (2):

(1) o, e

{ luò   落   (to fall)
{ lè   乐   (to laugh, glad)
{ luòlė   落了   (to have fallen)
{ lèlė   乐了   (to have laughed, to have been glad)
{ duó   夺   (to take by force)
{ dé   得   (to get)
{ duódào   夺到   (to have taken by force)
{ dédào   得到   (to have got)

(2) an, en

{ pán   盘   (plate)
{ pén   盆   (basin)
{ pánzi   盘子   (plate)
{ pénzi   盆子   (basin)

{ zhān	沾	(to soil)
{ zhēn	眞	(really, real)
{ zhānde	沾的	(soiled)
{ zhēnde	眞的	(real, genuine)

(3) ang, eng

{ bàng	磅	(pound, to weigh)
{ bèng	蹦	(to hop, to jump)
{ bàngyíbàng	磅一磅	(to weigh once or for a little while)
{ bèngyíbèng	蹦一蹦	(to jump once or for a little while)
{ fāng	方	(square)
{ fēng	風	(wind)
{ dōngfāng	东方	(the east)
{ dōngfēng	东風	(east wind)

(4) an, ang

{ mán	蛮	(wild, barbaric)
{ máng	忙	(busy)
{ mánjíle	蛮極了	(extremely wild)
{ mángjíle	忙極了	(extremely busy)
{ tān	貪	(greed)
{ tāng	湯	(soup)
{ tānduō	貪多	(greedy)
{ tāngduō	湯多	(much soup)

(5) en, eng

{ fén	粉	(powder)
{ féng	諷	(to ridicule)
{ féncì	粉刺	(pimple)
{ féngcì	諷刺	(to ridicule, ridicule)
{ shēn	深	(deep)
{ shēng	生	(to give birth to, strange)
{ shēnshuǐ	深水	(deep water)
{ shēngshuǐ	生水	(unboiled water)

(6) s, sh

{ sì	四	(four)
{ shí	十	(ten)
{ sìshí	四十	(forty)
{ shísì	十四	(fourteen)

sān	三	(three)
shān	山	(hill)
sānlǐ	三里	(three "li")
shānlǐ	山里	(among the hills)

(7) z, c

zuò	作	(to do)
cuò	錯	(mistaken)
méizuò	沒作	(did not do)
méicuò	沒錯	(not mistaken)
zǎor	棗兒	(dates)
cǎor	草兒	(grass)
xiǎozǎor	小棗兒	(little dates)
xiǎocǎor	小草兒	(little grass)

(8) c, s

cì	刺	(to sting)
sì	寺	(abbey)
yígècì	一個刺	(one sting)
yígèsì	一個寺	(one abbey)
cāi	猜	(to guess)
sāi	塞	(to stop, to fill up)
cāiyìcāi	猜一猜	(to make a guess)
sāiyìsāi	塞一塞	(to stop)

(9) i, ü

yìjiàn	意見	(opinion)
yùjiàn	遇見	(to meet)
méiyǒuyìjiàn	沒有意見	(no opinion)
méiyǒuyùjiàn	沒有遇見	(did not meet)
qī	期	(period)
qū	曲	(curved)
qīxiàn	期限	(limit of time)
qūxiàn	曲綫	(curve)

3) Pay attention to the basic strokes of the following components of Chinese characters and copy them.

1	八	丿 八
2	刀	𠃌 刀
3	臼	丿 亻 𠂤 𠂤 臼 臼
4	儿	丿 儿
5	田	丨 冂 冂 用 田
6	凵	𠃊 凵
7	夬	𠃌 二 ヨ 夬
8	方	丶 亠 方 方
9	夂	丿 𠂊 夂 夂
10	灬	丶 丷 灬 灬

Home Work

1) Read correctly the words or word groups containing retroflex vowels in the exercises of this lesson.

2) Read as many times as possible the difficult sounds in pairs in the exercises of this lesson.

3) Copy five times the components of Chinese characters in this lesson.

Oral Exercises

Lesson 9

Shēngcí 生詞 New Words

SIDE THREE, BAND FOUR

1.	nǐ	你	you
2.	hǎo	好	well, good
3.	qǐng	請	please
4.	jìn	进	to come in, to enter
5.	zuò	坐	to sit (down)
6.	xièxiê	謝謝	thanks
7.	shì	是	to be
8.	něi	哪	which
9.	guó	国	country
10.	rén	人	person, man
11.	wǒ	我	I, me
12.	Yīngguó	英国	Great Britain
13.	huì	会	can
14.	shuō	說	to speak, to say
15.	zhōngwén	中文	the Chinese language
16.	mā	嗎	(an interrogative particle)
17.	bù	不	not, no
18.	yīngwén	英文	English
19.	tā	他	he, him
20.	Zhōngguó	中国	China
21.	jiào	叫	to call, to be called
22.	shénmǒ	什么	what
23.	míngzì	名字	name

Duǎnjù 短句 Simple Sentences

SIDE THREE, BAND FOUR

(1) Nǐ hǎo!

你 好! How are you?

(2) Nǐ hǎo.

你 好! How are you?

(3) Qǐng jìn!

請 进! Come in, please.

(4) Qǐng zuò!

請 坐! Sit down, please!

(5) Xièxiè.

謝謝. Thanks.

(6) Nǐ shì něiguó rén?

你 是 哪国 人? Where do you come from?

(7) Wǒ shì Yīngguó rén.

我 是 英国 人. I am an Englishman.

(8) Nǐ huì shuō zhōngwén mā?

你 会 說 中文 嗎? Do you speak Chinese?

(9) Bú huì, wǒ shuō yīngwén.

不 会, 我 說 英文. No, I speak English.

(10) Tā shì něiguó rén?

他 是 哪国 人? Where does he come from?

(11) Tā shì Zhōngguó rén.

他 是 中国 人. He is Chinese.

(12) Nǐ jiào shénmǒ míngzì?

你 叫 什么 名字? What is your name?

(13) Wǒ jiào ——.

我 叫 ——. My name is____.

(14) Tā jiào shénmŏ míngzî?

他 叫 什么 名字？   What is his name?

(15) Tā jiào ——.

他 叫 ——.   His name is____.

Hànzì zìsù   汉字字素

Components of Chinese Characters

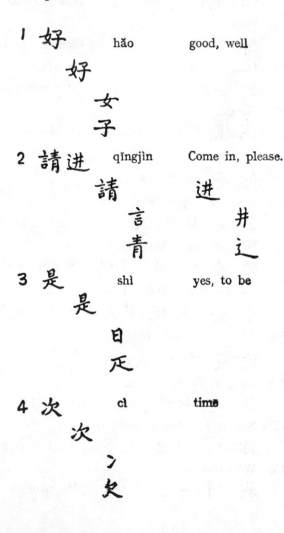

1 好   hǎo   good, well

好

女
子

2 請进   qǐngjìn   Come in, please.

請   进

言   丬
青   之

3 是   shì   yes, to be

是

日
疋

4 次   cì   time

次

ン
欠

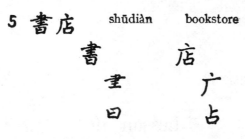

5 書店   shūdiàn   bookstore

書   店
   畫   广
   日   占

Jīběn bǐhuà   基本笔划
Basic Strokes

1	女	ノ く 女 女
2	言	、 一 亠 言 言
3	青	一 二 丰 主 青 青 青 青
4	丰	一 二 丰 丰
5	辶	、 辶 辶
6	疋	一 丁 下 疋 疋
7	冫	、 冫
8	欠	⺈ ⺈ 欠 欠
9	畫	⺆ ⺕ 田 聿 聿 畫
10	广	、 亠 广
11	占	丨 卜 占

Lesson 10

Shēngcí 生詞 New Words

SIDE FOUR, BAND ONE

1.	shéi	誰	who
2.	xuéshēng	学生	student
3.	xiānshēng	先生	teacher
4.	yǒu	有	to have, there is (are)
5.	kè	課	lesson, class
6.	méiyǒu	没有	to have no..., to have none, not to have...
7.	xiàwǔ	下午	afternoon
8.	fǔdǎo	輔导	to help...to study
9.	zài	在	at, in, on
10.	nǎr	哪兒	where
11.	wǒmēndė	我們的	our, ours
12.	jiàoshǐ	教室	classroom
13.	jǐ	几	how many
14.	diǎnzhōng	点鐘	hour
15.	kāishǐ	开始	to begin, to start
16.	sāndiǎn	三点	three o'clock
17.	bàn	半	half
18.	xuéxí	学習	to learn
19.	Běidà	北大	Peking University
20.	yě	也	also, too

Duǎnjù 短句 Simple Sentences
SIDE FOUR, BAND ONE

(1) Tā shì shéi?

他 是 誰? Who is he?

(2) Tā shì xuéshēng.

他 是 学生. He is a student.

(3) Tā shì shéi?

他 是 誰? Who is he?

(4) Tā shì xiānshēng.

他 是 先生. He is a teacher.

(5) Nǐ yǒu kè mǎ?

你 有 課 嗎? Do you have classes?

(6) Yǒu kè.

有 課. I do.

(7) Méi yǒu.

沒 有. I don't.

(8) Nǐ xiàwǔ yǒu kè mǎ?

你 下午 有 課 嗎? Do you have classes in the afternoon?

(9) Méi yǒu kè, yǒu fǔdǎo.

沒 有 課, 有 輔导. I don't, but my teacher will come to help me study.

(10) Zài nǎr fǔdǎo?

在 哪兒 輔导? Where will your teacher come to help you?

(11) Zài wǒmēndē jiàoshǐ.

在 我們的 教室. In our classroom.

(12) Jǐ diǎnzhōng kāishǐ fǔdǎo?

几 点鐘 开始 輔导? When will your teacher come to help you?

(13) Sāndiǎn bàn.

三点 半. Half past three.

(14) Nǐ zài nǎr xuéxí?

你 在 哪兒 学習? Where are you studying?

(15) Wǒ   zài   Běidà   xuéxí.
我 在 北大 学习.   I am studying in Peking University.

(16) Tā   zài   nǎr   xuéxí?
他 在 哪兒 学习?   Where is he studying?

(17) Tā   yě   zài   Běidà   xuéxí.
他 也 在 北大 学习.   He is also studying in Peking University.

Hànzì zìsù   汉字字素
Components of Chinese Characters

1 誰   shéi   who

　誰

　言
　隹

2 沿   yán   along

　沿

　氵 几
　口

3 疼   téng   painful

　疼
　广 夂
　冫

4 新的   xīndė   new (one)

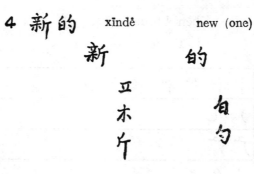

新

　　立
　　木
　　斤

的

　　白
　　勺

5 草   cǎo   grass

草

　　卝
　　曰
　　十

6 外边   wàibiān   outside

外

　　夕
　　卜

边

　　力
　　辶

Jīběn bǐhuà 基本笔划
Basic Strokes

1	佳	亻 亻 亻 佇 佇 佳 佳
2	几	丿 几
3	疒	广 疒
4	夂	丿 夂 夂
5	立	丶 二 亠 立 立
6	木	一 十 才 木
7	斤	丿 亻 斤 斤
8	北	丶 丬 丬 北
9	十	一 十
10	夕	丿 夕 夕
11	卜	丨 卜
12	力	𠃌 力

Lesson 11

Shēngcí 生詞 New Words

SIDE FOUR, BAND TWO

1.	shàngkè	上課	to have classes, to go to classes
2.	lē	了	(a modal particle)
3.	hái	还	still, yet
4.	nē	呢	(a modal particle)
5.	wèntí	問題	question, problem
6.	dǒnglē	懂了	to have understood
7.	duìlē	对了	right
8.	nán	难	difficult
9.	dàshēng	大声	loudly, aloud
10.	zài	再	again, once more
11.	niàn	念	to read
12.	yíbiàn	一遍	one time, once
13.	xiě	写	to write
14.	dàjiā	大家	all (the people)
15.	yíkuàir	一塊兒	together
16.	gēn	跟	with, after, to follow
17.	tīng	听	to hear, to listen
18.	wèn	問	to ask, to inquire
19.	huídá	回答	to answer

20. xiàkè 下課 the class is over, after class
21. zàijiàn 再見 good-bye

Duǎnjù 短句 Simple Sentences
SIDE FOUR, BAND TWO

(1) Shàng kè lė mȧ?
上 課 了 嗎? Is it time for class?

(2) Shàng kè lė.
上 課 了. It is.

(3) Hái méi yǒu nė!
还 沒 有 呢! Not yet.

(4) Nǐ yǒu wèntí mȧ?
你 有 問題 嗎? Have you any question?

(5) Yǒu.
有. Yes, I have.

(6) Méi yǒu.
沒 有. No, I have none.

(7) Nǐ dǒng lė mȧ?
你 懂 了 嗎? Do you understand?

(8) Dǒng lė.
懂 了. I do.

(9) Bù dǒng.
不 懂. I don't.

(10) Duì lė mȧ?
对 了 嗎? Is it right?

(11) Duì lė.
对 了. It is right.

(12) Bú duì.
不 对. No, it isn't.

(13) Nán bù nán?
难 不 难? Is it difficult?

(14) Nán.
难. It is.

(15) Bù nán.

不 难.

No, it isn't.

(16) Qǐng nǐ niàn.

请 你 念.

Please read.

(17) Qǐng nǐ dà shēng niàn.

请 你 大 声 念.

Please read loudly.

(18) Qǐng nǐ zài niàn yíbiàn.

请 你 再 念 一遍.

Please read it once more.

(19) Qǐng nǐ xiě.

请 你 写.

Please write.

(20) Qǐng nǐ zài xiě yíbiàn.

请 你 再 写 一遍.

Please write it once more.

(21) Dàjiā yíkuàir niàn.

大家 一块兒 念.

All of you read together.

(22) Dàjiā gēn wǒ niàn.

大家 跟 我 念.

All of you read after me.

(23) Wǒ niàn, nǐmen tīng.

我 念, 你們 听.

I'll read, and will you please listen.

(24) Wǒ shuō, nǐmen xiě.

我 說, 你們 写.

I'll speak, and will you please write it down.

(25) Wǒ wèn, nǐmen huídá.

我 問, 你們 回答.

I'll ask and you'll answer.

(26) Hǎo, xià kè le, zàijiàn!

好, 下 課 了, 再見!

All right, class is over, good-bye!

(27) Zàijiàn!

再見!

Good-bye!

Hànzì zìsù 汉字字素
Components of Chinese Characters

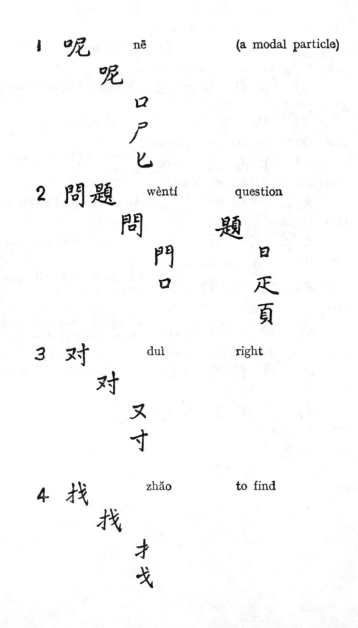

1 呢   nē   (a modal particle)

2 問題   wèntí   question

3 对   duì   right

4 找   zhǎo   to find

5 知道   zhīdǎo   to know

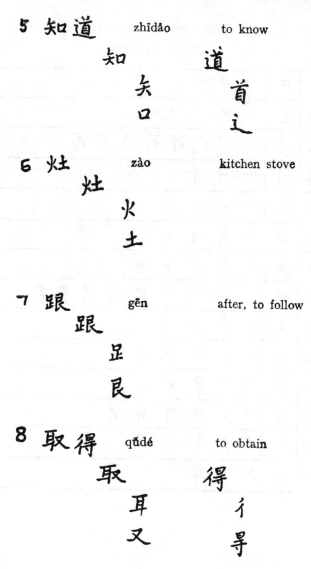

6 灶   zào   kitchen stove

7 跟   gēn   after, to follow

8 取得   qǔdé   to obtain

Jīběn bǐhuà   基本笔划
Basic Strokes

1	尸	フ コ 尸
2	匕	ノ 匕
3	頁	一 丆 丆 百 百 百 頁
4	寸	一 十 寸
5	才	一 十 才
6	戈	一 弋 弋 戈
7	矢	ノ ㇌ 二 午 矢
8	首	丶 丷 丷 䒑 产 芒 肖 首 首
9	火	丶 丿 丿 火
10	足	口 マ 尸 足 足
11	艮	フ コ ヨ 尸 艮 艮
12	耳	一 丆 丌 丌 耳 耳
13	彳	ノ ㇒ 彳
14	帚	彐 彐 帚

Lesson 12

Shēngcí 生詞 New Words

SIDE FOUR, BAND THREE

1.	tóngzhì	同志	comrade
2.	dào	到	to go (to), to arrive
3.	qù	去	to go
4.	shítáng	食堂	dining hall, refectory
5.	túshūguǎn	圖書館	library
6.	hézuòshè	合作社	co-operative store
7.	yào	要	to want
8.	mǎi	买	to buy
9.	dōngxi	东西	thing
10.	běnzi	本子	note-book
11.	qiānbǐ	鉛笔	pencil
12.	shū	書	book
13.	hé	和	and
14.	zhǐ	紙	paper
15.	duōshǎo	多少	how many, how much
16.	qián	錢	money
17.	liǎng	两	two
18.	máo	毛	ten cents
19.	wǔ	五	five
20.	yī	一	one
21.	kuài	塊	dollar (a measure word)
22.	jìnchéng	进城	to go to the city
23.	sùshè	宿舍	dormitory

24. xiànzài   現在   now
25. huí   回   to return

Duǎnjù   短句   Simple Sentences

SIDE FOUR, BAND THREE

(1) Tóngzhì! nǐ dào nǎr qù?
同志! 你 到 哪兒 去?
Comrade! Where are you going?

(2) Wǒ dào shítáng qù.
我 到 食堂 去.
I am going to the dining hall.

(3) Wǒ huí sùshè qù.
我 回 宿舍 去.
I am returning to the dormitory.

(4) Tā dào nǎr qù?
他 到 哪兒 去?
Where is he going?

(5) Tā dào túshūguǎn qù.
他 到 圖書館 去.
He is going to the library.

(6) Nǐ qù hézuòshè må?
你 去 合作社 嗎?
Are you going to the co-operative store?

(7) Qù.
去.
Yes, I am.

(8) Bú qù.
不 去.
No, I am not.

(9) Nǐ yào mǎi shénmå dōngxi?
你 要 买 什么 东西?
What do you want to buy?

(10) Wǒ yào mǎi běnzi.
我 要 买 本子.
I want to buy note-books.

(11) Wǒ yào mǎi qiānbǐ.
我 要 买 鉛笔.
I want to buy pencils.

(12) Tā yào mǎi shénmå dōngxi?
他 要 买 什么 东西?
What does he want to buy?

(13) Tā yào mǎi shū hé zhǐ.
他 要 买 書 和 紙.
He wants to buy books and paper.

(14) Běnzi   duōshǎo   qián?

本子 多少 錢？

How much is the note-book?

(15) Liǎngmáo wǔ.

两毛 五.

Twenty-five cents.

(16) Shū   duōshǎo   qián?

書 多少 錢？

How much is the book?

(17) Yíkuài   qián.

一块 錢.

One dollar.

(18) Nǐ xiànzài jìn chéng mǎ?

你 现在 进 城 吗？

Are you going to the city now?

(19) Jìn   chéng.

进 城.

Yes, I am going to the city.

(20) Bú jìn   chéng.

不 进 城.

No, I am not going to the city.

Hànzì zìsù   汉字字素

Components of Chinese Characters

1 同志   tóngzhì   comrade

同
门
一
口

志
士
心

2 計划   jìhuà   plan

計
言
十

划
戈
刂

3　飯　　fàn　　　　　　meal

飯
食
反

4　合作社　hézuòshè　co-operative store

合　　作　　社
人　　亻　　礻
一　　乍　　土
口

5　袖子　xiùzi　　　sleeve

袖　子
礻　子
由

6　鉛笔　qiānbǐ　　pencil

鉛　笔
金　竹
几　毛
口

7　紙　zhǐ　　paper

紙
糹
氏

8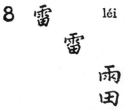

Jīběn bǐhuà 基本笔划
Basic Strokes

1	冂	丨 冂
2	士	十 士
3	心	丶 心 心 心
4	刂	丶 刂
5	食	丿 𠆢 卜 𠂉 𠆢 合 食 食
6	反	丿 厂 反
7	人	丿 人
8	乍	丿 亻 亼 乍 乍
9	衤	丶 ㇇ 衤 衤
10	木	木 木
11	金	人 亼 仐 全 金 金
12	竹	丿 ㇒ 午 竹 竹 竹
13	毛	丿 ㇒ 三 毛
14	糸	㇈ 幺 幺 糸 糸 糸
15	氏	丿 亻 ㇄ 氏
16	雨	一 厂 冂 雨 雨 雨 雨 雨

Basic Grammar

Abbreviations Adopted in the Words Columns

（名）	名　詞　Míngcí The Noun
（代）	代　詞　Dàicí The Pronoun
（动）	动　詞　Dòngcí The Verb
（能动）	能願动詞　néngyuàndòngcí The Optative Verb
（数）	数　詞　Shùcí The Numeral
（形）	形容詞　Xíngróngcí The Adjective
（介）	介　詞　Jièci The Preposition
（副）	副　詞　Fùcí The Adverb
（連）	連　詞　Liáncí The Conjunction
（嘆）	嘆　詞　Tàncí The Interjection
（助）	助　詞　Zhùcí The Particle
（头）	詞　头　Cítóu The Prefix
（尾）	詞　尾　Cíwěi The Suffix

Lesson 13

生詞 Shēngcí New Words
SIDE FOUR, BAND FOUR

1.	这	(代)	zhèi, zhè	this
2.	是	(动)	shì	to be
3.	書	(名)	shū	book
4.	我	(代)	wǒ	I, me
5.	学生	(名)	xuéshēng	student
6.	先生	(名)	xiānshēng	teacher, Mr, sir
7.	中国	(名)	Zhōngguó	China, Chinese
8.	人	(名)	rén	man, person
9.	那	(代)	nèi, nà	that
10.	不	(副)	bù	not, no
11.	你	(代)	nǐ	you
12.	吗	(助)	mā	(an interrogative particle)
13.	您	(代)	nín	(the polite form of 你)
14.	报	(名)	bào	newspaper
15.	他	(代)	tā	he, him

語法 Yǔfǎ Grammar

13.1 The Sentence with a Substantive Predicate (1) In modern Chinese, sentences may be divided into four kinds, according to the construction of the predicate. The first kind is the sentence with a substantive predicate. Here we will deal with the sentence with a substantive predicate (1).

A sentence, in which the main element of the predicate is made up of a substantive, is called the sentence with a substantive predicate (1). The substantive may be a noun, a pronoun, or a numeral; it tells "what" the person or thing is as required by the subject. The copula may be looked upon as a particular verb used to connect the subject with the substantive in the predicate. The predicate which is composed of a substantive and a copula must explain the subject. e. g.

1. 这　　是　　书.
   Zhèi　　shì　　shū.

   This is a book.

2. 我　　是　　学生.
   Wǒ　　shì　　xuéshěng.

   I am a student.

3. 先生　　是　　中国　　人.
   Xiānshěng　　shì　　Zhōngguó　　rén.

   The teacher is Chinese (LIT.: China person).

这, 我 , and 先生 are subjects; 是书, 是学生, and 是中国人 are predicates. All the words after the copula are nouns.

   13.2 The Negative Form of the Sentence with a Substantive Predicate (1)   The negative form of such kind of sentence is made by putting the negative adverb 不 before the copula 是. e. g.

4. 那　　不　　是　　书.
   Nèi　　bú　　shì　　shū.

   That is not a book.

5. 你　　不　　是　　先生.
   Nǐ　　bú　　shì　　xiānshěng.

   You are not a teacher.

6.
学生　　不　　是　　中国　　人.
Xuéshēng　bú　shì　Zhōngguó　rén.

The student is not Chinese.

The adverb 不 is pronounced in the 4th tone when it is used independently or followed by a syllable of the 1st, 2nd or 3rd tone; but it is pronounced in the 2nd tone when it is followed by a syllable of the 4th tone. Hence, in the above three examples, 不 is in the 2nd tone.

13.3 The Interrogative Sentence (1)   In modern Chinese, there are five kinds of interrogative sentences that are frequently used. Here, we will deal with the first kind. When we put the interrogative modal particle 嗎 at the end of a declarative sentence (affirmative or negative), it is changed into an interrogative sentence. e. g.

7. 这　　是　　書　　嗎?
Zhèi　shì　shū　mǎ?

Is this a book?

8. 这　　不　　是　　書　　嗎?
Zhèi　bú　shì　shū　mǎ?

Isn't this a book?

13.4 你 and 您   你 and 您 are both in the second person singular. But 您 is a polite form, and used only when we wish to pay respect to the person in question. e. g.

9. 您　　不　　是　　学生,　　您　　是　　先生.
Nín　bú　shì　xuéshēng,　nín　shì　xiānshēng.

You (formal) are not a student, you are a teacher.

課文　Kèwén　Text

SIDE FOUR, BAND FOUR

I

1. 这　是　書.
Zhèi　shì　shū.
This is a book.

2. 那　是　报.
Nèi　shì　bào.
That is a newspaper.

3. 他　是　先生.
Tā　shì　xiānshēng.
He is the (OR a) teacher.

4. 我　是　学生.
Wǒ　shì　xuéshēng.
I am a student.

5. 先生　是　中国　人.
Xiānshēng　shì　Zhōngguó　rén.
The teacher is Chinese (LIT.: a China person).

II

6. 这　不　是　書.
Zhèi　bú　shì　shū.
This is not a book.

7. 那　不　是　报.
Nèi　bú　shì　bào.
That is not a newspaper.

8. 我　不　是　先生.
Wǒ　bú　shì　xiānshēng.
I am not the teacher.

9. 您　不　是　学生.
Nín　bú　shì　xuéshēng.
You (formal "you") are not a student.

10. 他　不　是　中国　人.
Tā　bú　shì　Zhōngguó rén.
He is not Chinese.

III

11. 这　是　书,　那　是　报.
Zhèi　shì　shū,　nèi　shì　bào.
This is a book, that is a newspaper.

12. 这　是　书,　这　不　是　报.
Zhèi　shì　shū,　zhèi　bú　shì　bào.
This is a book, this is not a newspaper.

13. 那　不　是　报,　那　是　书.
Nèi　bú　shì　bào,　nèi　shì　shū.
That is not a newspaper, that is a book.

14. 我　是　学生,　您　是　先生.
Wǒ　shì　xuéshēng,　nín　shì　xiānshēng.
I am a student, you (formal) are the teacher.

15. 他　不　是　先生,　他　是　学生.
Tā　bú　shì　xiānshēng,　tā　shì　xuéshēng.
He is not a teacher, he is a student.

IV

(a₁) 这　是　书　吗?
Zhèi　shì　shū　må?
Is this a book?

(b₁) 这　是　书.
Zhèi　shì　shū.
This is a book. (= Yes.)

(a₂) 那　是　报　吗?
Nèi　shì　bào　må?
Is that a newspaper?

(b₂) 那 不 是 报, 那 是 書.
Nèi bú shì bào, nèi shì shū.
That is not a newspaper, that is a book. (= No, that is a book.)

(a₃) 你 是 学生 嗎?
Nǐ shì xuéshēng mǎ?
Are you a student?

(b₃) 我 是 学生.
Wǒ shì xuéshēng.
I am a student. (= Yes.)

(a₄) 他 是 中国 人 嗎?
Tā shì Zhōngguó rén mǎ?
Is he Chinese?

(b₄) 他 不 是 中国 人.
Tā bú shì Zhōngguó rén.
He is not Chinese. (= No.)

課外練習 Kèwài liànxí Home Work

1) Copy all the new words once.

2) Transcribe the following sentences by using the phonetic alphabet and give the correct tone of each syllable:

(1) 我 是 学生.

(2) 他 不 是 先生.

(3) 这 是 書 嗎?

3) Answer the following questions with Chinese characters:

(4) 你 是 中国 人 嗎?

(5) 那 是 报 嗎?

汉字表　Hànzì biǎo　Chinese Characters

1	这	文（丶 一 ナ 文）
		辶
2	是	
3	書	
4	我	丿 二 千 千 我 我 我
5	学	𭕄（丶 丷 丷 丷 𭕄）
		子
6	生	丿 𠂉 仁 牛 生
7	先	丿 𠂉 丬 生 先
8	中	丶 冂 口 中
9	国	
10	人	
11	那	刅（刀 刃 刅）
		阝
12	不	一 丆 𠀙 不
13	你	
14	嗎	口
		馬（一 二 三 手 再 馬 馬）
15	您	你
		心

16	报	扌
		艮（ㄱ ㄕ 艮）
17	他	亻
		也（ㄱ ㄌ 也）

Lesson 14

生詞 Shēngcí New Words

SIDE FOUR, BAND FIVE

1.	一	(数) yī	a, one
2.	本	(量) běn	(a measure word)
3.	个	(量) gè	(a measure word)
4.	三	(数) sān	three
5.	很	(副) hěn	very
6.	新	(形) xīn	new
7.	好	(形) hǎo	good, well
8.	張	(量) zhāng	(a measure word)
9.	紙	(名) zhǐ [張]	paper
10.	小	(形) xiǎo	little, small
11.	大	(形) dà	big, large
12.	多	(形) duō	many, much
13.	少	(形) shǎo	few, little
14.	北京	(名) Běijīng	Peking
15.	旧	(形) jiù	old

語法 Yǔfǎ Grammar

14.1 **The Nominal Measure Word**   Persons, things and actions may all be numbered or weighed. The words showing the numerical or quantitative units of persons or things, are called nominal measure words; and those which indicate such units of actions are called verbal measure words. Here we will deal with the nominal measure words.

In modern Chinese, generally speaking, a numeral (such as 一) or a demonstrative pronoun (such as 这 and 那) cannot be directly used with a noun; a measure word should always be used between it and the noun. e. g.

1. 这 是 一本 书.
   Zhèi shì yìběn shū.
   This is a (one) book.

2. 那个 学生 是 中国 人.
   Nèige xuéshěng shì Zhōngguó rén.
   That student is Chinese.

We cannot say 一书 or 那学生, for after 一 and 那 there should be a measure word.

Many nouns have their specific measure words, for example, 本 is the specific measure word for 书. 个 is a very common measure word, and is most extensively used, for it may be used in connection with persons (e. g. the measure word of 学生 is 个.), and also in the case of things that have no specific measure words for themselves. It may even be substituted for other specific measure words.

The following four points should be observed in using measure words:

(1) When there are a demonstrative pronoun and a numeral before the measure word, the demonstrative pronoun should be put before the numeral. e. g.

3. 这 三个 学生
   zhèi sāngě xuéshěng
   these three students

4. 那 三本 书
   nèi sānběn shū
   those three books

(2) The measure word is directly annexed to the demonstrative pronoun or the numeral. e. g.

5. <u>这个</u> 学生
   zhèigè xuéshēng

   this student

6. <u>三本</u> 书
   sānběn shū

   three books

If there is no numeral or demonstrative pronoun, then no measure word can be allowed to stand alone before a noun. For instance, we can never say such a thing as 个先生是中国人.

(3) There are a few nouns which possess in themselves the nature or function of the measure word, and hence do not require measure words when they are preceded by numerals or demonstrative pronouns. e. g. 一年 (one year) and 这課 (this lesson).

(4) When the person or thing denoted by the noun is already clearly defined in the context, the noun after the measure word may be omitted. e. g.

7. 这个 中国 人 是 先生,
   Zhèigè Zhōngguó rén shì xiānshēng,

   那个 (中国 人) 是 学生.
   nèigè (Zhōngguó rén) shì xuéshēng.

   This Chinese is a teacher, that one (Chinese) is a student.

中国人 after 那个 may be omitted.

14.2 The Tones of 一 The tones of the numeral 一 vary:
(1) When it stands alone; or when reading a number of more than one figure, if one does not read the names of the decimal units, e. g. 1910 (一九一〇), 01521 (〇一五二一); or if 一 is the last figure of a number of more than one figure, e. g. 二十一 or 七百六十一, it is pronounced in the 1st tone.

(2) When it is followed by a syllable of the 1st, 2nd or 3rd tone, or by a syllable of the neutral tone that is originally in the 1st, 2nd or 3rd tone, it is pronounced in the 4th tone. e. g. yìzhāng zhǐ (a sheet of paper), yìtiáo lù (a way) and yìběn shū (a book).

(3) When it is followed by a syllable of the 4th tone, or by a syllable of the neutral tone that is originally in the 4th tone, it is pronounced in the 2nd tone. e. g. yígè rén (a person).

14.3 **The Sentence with an Adjectival Predicate**   A sentence, of which the predicate is composed of an adjective, is called the sentence with an adjectival predicate. An adjective is a word used to show the quality or appearance of a person or thing. Therefore, in a sentence with an adjectival predicate, the predicate is used to describe the quality, appearance and so forth of the person or thing denoted by the subject. In other words, the predicate tells us chiefly "how" is the person or thing denoted by the subject. e. g.

8. 这本　书　很　新.
   Zhèiběn　shū　hěn　xīn.

   This book is very new.

9. 那个　学生　很　好.
   Nèigè　xuéshēng　hěn　hǎo.

   That student is very good.

书 and 学生 are subjects. 新 and 好 are predicates. In the predicates, 很 is an adverb of degree, used as adverbial modifier modifying the adjectives 新 and 好.

If we wish to negate a sentence with an adjectival predicate, we simply put the negative adverb 不 before the adjective. e. g.

10. 这本　书　不　好.
    Zhèiběn　shū　bù　hǎo.

    This book is not good.

11. 那張　紙　不　小.
    Nèizhāng　zhǐ　bù　xiǎo.

    That (sheet of) paper is not small.

There are two points worth noticing concerning the sentence with an adjectival predicate:

(1) Before the adjectival predicate, the copula 是 is never used. This is a characteristic of Chinese syntax.

(2) The adverb 很 is often used before a simple predicative adjective in an affirmative declarative sentence. In such a case, it is very weak, having completely lost its significance as a word emphasizing degree (but it is not so in negative and

interrogative sentences). An adjectival predicate without such an adverbial modifier implies a sense of comparison, for instance, when we say 这本书新 it implies also 那本书旧. Therefore, such expressions are often used in comparisons. e. g.

12. 这張　紙　大，　那張　紙　小.
Zhèizhāng zhǐ dà, nèizhāng zhǐ xiǎo.

This sheet of paper is big, that sheet of paper is small.

13. 这本　書　好,　那本　書　不　好.
Zhèiběn shū hǎo, nèiběn shū bù hǎo.

This book is good, that book is not good.

14.4 多 and 少 多 and 少, two very common adjectives, may also be used as predicates. In such a case, either of them may be used alone as a predicate (implying comparison), and be preceded by an adverbial modifier. e. g.

14. 学生　多,　先生　少.
Xuéshēng duō, xiānshēng shǎo.

The students are many, the teachers are few.

15. 学生　很　多.
Xuéshēng hěn duō.

There are (very) many students.

16. 先生　很　少.
Xiānshēng hěn shǎo.

There are (very) few teachers.

But as adjective modifiers of nouns, they are different from other adjectives: we must say 很多 or 很少, though the word 很 is rather weak in meaning. We cannot say 多先生是北京人, but we must say:

17. 很　多　先生　是　北京　人.
Hěn duō xiānshēng shì Běijīng rén.

(Very) many teachers come from Peking (LIT.: are Peking people).

課文   Kèwén   Text

SIDE FOUR, BAND FIVE

I

1. 这 是 一本 書.
   Zhèi   shì   yìběn   shū.
   This is a (one) book.

2. 这 是 一張 紙, 那 是 一張 报.
   Zhèi   shì   yìzhāng   zhǐ,   nèi   shì   yìzhāng   bào.
   This is a sheet of paper, that is a (sheet of) newspaper.

3. 这張 紙 大, 那張 紙 小.
   Zhèizhāng   zhǐ   dà,   nèizhāng   zhǐ   xiǎo.
   This sheet of paper is big, that one (that sheet of paper) is little.

II

4. 这 是 一本 書.
   Zhèi   shì   yìběn   shū.
   This is a book.

5. 这本 書 很 新.
   Zhèiběn   shū   hěn   xīn.
   This book is (very) new.

6. 这本 書 新, 那本 書 旧.
   Zhèiběn   shū   xīn,   nèiběn   shū   jiù.
   This book is new, that book is old.

7. 这本 書 很 好.
   Zhèiběn   shū   hěn   hǎo.
   This book is (very) good.

8. 这本　书　好,　那本　书　不　好.
Zhèibĕn shū hǎo, nèibĕn shū bù hǎo.
This book is good, that book is not good.

III

9. 这　一个　中国　人　是　学生.
Zhèi yígĕ Zhōngguó rén shì xuéshĕng.
This (one) Chinese (person) is a student.

10. 这个　学生　很　好.
Zhèigĕ xuéshĕng hĕn hǎo.
This student is (very) good.

11. 很　多　学生　是　北京　人.
Hĕn duō xuéshĕng shì Bĕijīng rén.
Many students are from Peking (LIT.: are Peking people).

12. 那　一个　中国　人　是　先生.
Nèi yígĕ Zhōngguó rén shì xiānshĕng.
That Chinese is the (OR a) teacher.

13. 那个　先生　很　好.
Nèigĕ xiānshĕng hĕn hǎo.
That teacher is (very) good.

14. 很　多　先生　是　北京　人.
Hĕn duō xiānshĕng shì Bĕijīng rén.
Many teachers are from Peking.

IV

(a₁) 这　是　书　吗?
Zhèi shì shū mǎ?
Is this a book?

(b₁)   这 不 是 书, 那 是 书.
Zhèi bú shì shū, nèi shì shū.

This is not a book, that is a book.

(a₂)   那本 书 好 吗?
Nèiběn shū hǎo må?

Is that book good?

(b₂)   那本 书 不 好, 这本 书 好.
Nèiběn shū bù hǎo, zhèiběn shū hǎo.

That book is not good, this book is good.

(a₃)   很 多 先生 是 北京 人 吗?
Hěn duō xiānshēng shì Běijīng rén må?

Are many teachers from Peking?

(b₃)   很 多 先生 是 北京 人.
Hěn duō xiānshēng shì Běijīng rén.

Many teachers are from Peking. (=Yes.)

(a₄)   很 多 学生 是 北京 人 吗?
Hěn duō xuéshēng shì Běijīng rén må?

Are many students from Peking?

(b₄)   很 多 学生 是 北京 人.
Hěn duō xuéshēng shì Běijīng rén.

Many students are from Peking. (=Yes.)

課外練習   Kèwài liànxí   Home Work

1) Copy all the new words in this lesson once.

2) Change the following phonetic spellings into Chinese characters:

(1) Xuéshēng hěn duō.
(2) Bào hěn shǎo.

3) Copy and fill these blanks with proper measure words:

(3)   这 是 一____ 纸.

(4) 那＿＿　書　很　好.

(5) 那＿＿　学生　是　中国　人　嗎?

4) Translate and answer the following questions:
  (6) Is that sheet of paper big ?
  (7) Is that book old ?
  (8) Is this Chinese the new teacher ?

汉字表　Hànzì biǎo　Chinese Characters

1	一	
2	本	木 本
3	个	人 个
4	三	一 二 三
5	很	彳
		艮
6	新	
7	好	
8	張	弓（フ ㄱ 弓）
		長（一 Ｔ Ｆ Ｅ 長 長 長 長）
9	紙	
10	小	
11	大	一 ナ 大
12	多	夕
		夕

13	少	小 少
14	北	丨 丬 ⺬ 北 北
15	京	丶 亠 古 京
16	旧	丨 旧

Lesson 15

生詞　Shēngcí　New Words

1.	的	(助)	dē	(a structural particle)
2.	同志	(名)	tóngzhì	comrade
3.	俄文	(名)	èwén	the Russian language
4.	朋友	(名)	péngyǒu	friend
5.	干淨	(形)	gānjìng	clean
6.	我們	(代)	wǒmén	we, us
7.	你們	(代)	nǐmén	you
8.	他們	(代)	tāmén	they, them
9.	她	(代)	tā	she, her
10.	它	(代)	tā	it
11.	枝	(量)	zhī	(a measure word)
12.	鉛笔	(名)	qiānbǐ [枝]	pencil
13.	長	(形)	cháng	long
14.	短	(形)	duǎn	short
15.	黑板	(名)	hēibǎn	blackboard

語法　Yǔfǎ　Grammar

15.1 The Structural Particle 的 (1) We know already that adjectives may modify nouns, an adjective modifier is an adjective modifying a noun (14.4), and the noun modified is called the central word. Besides adjectives, nouns, pronouns and words of other parts of speech and even constructions (phrases) may all be used as adjective modifiers. Here in this lesson we will consider nouns, pronouns and adjectives used as adjective modifiers. An adjective modifier must precede the central word or the word it modifies, and the structural particle 的 is often used in between. e. g.

1. 先生的　書　很　多.
   Xiānshěngdě　shū　hěn　duō.

   The teacher has very many books. (LIT.: The teacher's books are very many.)

2. 这　是　他的　紙.
   Zhèi　shì　tādě　zhǐ.

   This is his paper.

3. 他　是　一个　很　好的　同志.
   Tā　shì　yígě　hěn　hǎodě　tóngzhì.

   He is a very good comrade.

書, 紙, and 同志 are central words, 先生, 他 and 好 are adjective modifiers; there exists between the adjective modifier and the central word a relation of ownership (as in examples 1, 2) or a descriptive relationship (as in example 3). An adjective modifier of ownership can only be formed by a noun or a pronoun, while an adjective modifier made up of an adjective is always used to modify or describe the central word.

It is not quite true that after an adjective modifier there must be a structural particle 的. From the following rules we see when it has to be used or when not.

(1) Some nouns and pronouns used as adjective modifiers are so integral a part of their central words that they have become stable word groups. In such cases, we do not use the particle 的. e. g.

4. 中国　人
   Zhōngguó　rén

   (a) Chinese (person)

5. 俄文　报
   èwén　bào

   (a) Russian newspaper

6. 我　朋友
   wǒ　péngyǒu

   my friend

(2) When adjectives, especially monosyllabic ones, are used as adjective modifiers, we do not use the particle 的 in general. e. g.

7. 好　学生
   hǎo　xuéshēng

   (a) good student

8. 旧　书
   jiù　shū

   (an) old book

9. 干淨　纸
   gānjing　zhǐ

   clean paper

But, when the adjective is modified by an adverbial modifier, the particle 的 is generally indispensable (the adjectives 多 and 少 are exceptions). e. g.

10. 很　旧的　报
    hěn　jiùdě　bào

    (a) very old newspaper

11. 不　好的　书
    bù　hǎodě　shū

    (a) book that is not good

12. 很　干淨的　纸
    hěn　gānjingdě　zhǐ

    very clean paper

(3) When it is clear from the context what the central word should be, the central word may be omitted, but the particle 的 must on no account be left out after the adjective modifier. e. g.

13. 这本 新 书 干净, 那本 旧的 不 干净.
    Zhèiběn xīn shū gānjìng, nèiběn jiùdé bù gānjìng.

This new book is clean, that old one is not clean.

We say 旧的 instead of 旧书, because the idea of 书 is already expressed by 新书.

15.2 The Arrangement of Adjective Modifiers   Numerals in conjunction with measure words used before nouns (such as 一本书) and demonstrative pronouns in conjunction with measure words or with numerals and measure words used before nouns (such as 这本书 and 这三本书) are also adjective modifiers (with the exception of nouns used as measure words, all measure words are used without 的). When an adjective modifier is composed of a demonstrative pronoun, a numeral and a measure word, the demonstrative pronoun stands first, then the numeral and the measure word (14.1). When the modifier contains not only the three elements mentioned above, but also a personal pronoun, a noun or an adjective, the word order is as follows:

(1) In an adj. modifier, the adjective should be near the central word. e. g.

14. 那   一本   新   书
    nèi   yìběn   xīn   shū
    that new book

15. 这   一張   旧   报
    zhèi   yìzhāng   jiù   bào
    this old newspaper

(2) The personal pronoun must always stand before the demonstrative pronoun, therefore an adjective modifier of ownership composed of a personal pronoun or a noun must always come first. e. g.

16. <u>他的</u>　那　一張　旧　报
　　<u>tādĕ</u>　　nèi　yìzhāng　jiù　bào

that old newspaper of his (LIT.: his that one sheet old newspaper)

17. <u>先生的</u>　这　一本　新　書
　　<u>xiānshĕngdĕ</u>　zhèi　yìbĕn　xīn　shū

this new book of the teacher's

15.3 The Interrogative Sentence (2)　　The second kind of the interrogative sentence is alternative in form, including both the affirmative and the negative sides of a thing set side by side; in other words, the alternative form includes both the affirmative and the negative forms of the predicate. The person trying to answer the question is expected to choose between the two.　In the sentence with a substantive predicate (1), the alternative form is 是不是. e. g.

18. 他　是　不　是　先生?
　　Tā　shì　bú　shì　xiānshêng?

Is he a teacher? (LIT.: He is, not is, a teacher?)

19. 这　是　不　是　报?
　　Zhèi　shì　bú　shì　bào?

Is this a newspaper (or isn't it)?

不是 may also stand at the end of a sentence .c. g.

20. 他　是　先生　<u>不　是</u>?
　　Tā　shì　xiānshêng　<u>bú　shì?</u>

Is he a teacher? (LIT.: He is a teacher, not is?)

21. 这　是　报　<u>不　是</u>?
　　Zhèi　shì　bào　<u>bú　shì?</u>

Is this a newspaper?

In the sentence with an adjectival predicate, the alternative form includes both the affirmative and the negative forms of the predicative adjective. e. g.

22. 这本 書 好 不 好?
Zhèiběn shū hǎo bù hǎo?
Is this book good (or not)?

23. 那張 紙 干淨 不 干淨?
Nèizhāng zhǐ gānjǐng bù gānjǐng?
Is that paper clean (or not)?

15.4 們 們 is a suffix indicating plural number. All singular personal pronouns with 們 are plural in number. e. g.

24. 我——我們
wǒ——wǒmén

I ----- we (OR: me ----- us)

25. 你——你們
nǐ —— nǐmén

you (singular) --- you (plural)

(們 is, in general, not used after 您 to indicate plural number.)

26. 他——他們
tā —— tāmén

he ---- they (OR: him ---- them)

"們" may also be used after nouns indicating plural number, but attention should be paid to the following two points:

(1) 們 is only used after nouns denoting persons, such as 先生們, 学生們 etc. The other nouns cannot take such a suffix. We cannot say 書們, 报們 etc.

(2) A noun followed by the suffix 們 is always plural, but a noun without such a suffix may be either singular or plural. When it is clearly shown by context that the noun is in the plural, it is no longer necessary to use the suffix. e. g.

27. 我們 是 学生.
Wǒmén shì xuéshēng.
We are students.

28. <u>很 多</u> 先生 是 北京 人.

Hěn duō xiānshēng shì Běijing rén.

(Very) many teachers are from Peking.

Because 我們 and 很多 already imply that 学生, 先生 and 北京 人 are in the plural, we no longer use the suffix 們. According to the above, 們 is used only when there is absolute necessity and when there is no other indication of plurality.

15.5 她 **and** 它 These two words have the same pronunciation as 他, and are also pronouns of the third person singular. In writing, 他 may be used to indicate any person or thing of the third person singular. But now we always use 他 to denote the male, 她 the female and 它 all things or matters exclusive of human beings. 她 is the same as 他 in use, but 它 should never be used at the beginning of a sentence. We can say 她是先生, but we must never say 它是紙. Moreover, the word 它 cannot, in general, be followed by 們 to indicate plural number.

課文 Kèwén Text

SIDE FOUR, BAND SIX

I

1. 我 朋友的 書 很 多.

Wǒ péngyǒudě shū hěn duō.

My friend has many books. (LIT.: My friend's books are very many.)

2. 她的 書 很 新.

Tādě shū hěn xīn.

Her books are (very) new.

II

3. 这 是 一枝 新 鉛笔.

Zhèi shì yìzhī xīn qiānbǐ.

This is a new pencil.

4.   这枝　鉛笔　很　長.
Zhèizhī　qiānbǐ　hěn　cháng.
This pencil is (very) long.

5.   新　鉛笔　長,　旧　鉛笔　短.
Xīn　qiānbǐ　cháng, jiù　qiānbǐ　duǎn.
The new pencil is long, the old pencil is short.

III

(a_1)   这　是　黑板　不　是?
Zhèi　shì　hēibǎn　bú　shì?

Is this a blackboard (or is it not)?

(b_1)   这　是　黑板.
Zhèi　shì　hēibǎn.

This is a blackboard. (= Yes.)

(a_2)   这个　黑板　干淨　不　干淨?
Zhèigě　hēibǎn　gānjìng　bù　gānjìng?

Is this blackboard clean (or not clean)?

(b_2)   很　干淨,　这　是　一个　新
Hěn　gānjìng,　zhèi　shì　yígě　xīn
黑板.新的　干淨,　旧的　不
hēibǎn. Xīndě　gānjìng,　jiùdě　bù
干淨.
gānjìng.

(It is) very clean; this is a new blackboard. The new one is clean, the old one is not.

(a_3)   你們的　先生　是　中国　人　嗎?
Nǐměndě　xiānshěng　shì　Zhōngguó　rén　mǎ?

Is your teacher Chinese?

(b_3)   是　中国　人.
Shì　Zhōngguó　rén.

Yes. (LIT.: Is Chinese.)

(a₄) 你們的　　先生　多　不　多？
Nǐmĕndĕ　xiānshĕng　duō　bù　duō?

Do you have many teachers? (LIT.: Your teachers many not many?)

(b₄) 很　多.
Hĕn　duō.

Yes.

(a₅) 那个　　同志　是　不　是　你們的
Nèigĕ　tóngzhì　shì　bú　shì　nǐmĕndĕ
先生？
xiānshĕng?

Is that comrade your teacher?

(b₆) 是，她　是　我們的　　先生. 她　很
Shì,　tā　shì　wŏmĕndĕ　xiānshĕng. Tā　hĕn
好，她　是　一个　很　好的　先生.
hăo,　tā　shì　yígĕ　hĕn　hăodĕ　xiānshĕng.

Yes, she is our teacher. She is very good; she is a very good teacher.

課外練習　Kèwài liànxí　Home Work

1) Copy all the new words once.

2) The following words and word groups can all be used as adjective modifiers of nouns, so please fill the blanks with proper nouns (pay attention to the use and omission of the particle 的):

(1) 她們＿＿＿　(2) 朋友＿＿＿　(3) 旧 ＿＿＿
(4) 干淨＿＿＿　(5) 很 長＿＿＿　(6) 不 好＿＿＿

3) Change the following questions into alternative interrogative sentences, and write answers to all of them:

(7) 这个　黑板　大　嗎？

(8) 那 是 先生的 紙 嗎?

(9) 他 那枝 鉛笔 長 嗎?

(10) 您的 那个 朋友 是 一个 新 学生 嗎?

五、汉字表   Hànzì biǎo   Chinese Characters

1	的	
2	同	
3	志	
4	俄	亻
		我
5	文	
6	朋	月（） 丿 月 月)
		月
7	友	一 ナ 友
8	干	一 干
9	淨	氵
		爭（丿 𠂊 𠂊 𠂎 乌 乌 当 爭）
10	們	
11	她	女
		也

12	它	宀
		匕
13	枝	木
		支（十 支 ）
14	鉛	
15	笔	
16	長	
17	短	矢
		豆（一 口 戸 豆 豆 ）
18	黑	丶 冂 冂 冋 四 四 甲 里 黑
19	板	木
		反

Lesson 16

生詞 Shēngcí New Words
SIDE FOUR, BAND SEVEN

1. 工作　　（动、名）gōngzuò　to work, work
2. 学習　　（动）xuéxí　to study
3. 教　　　（动）jiāo　to teach
4. 中文　　（名）zhōngwén　the Chinese language
5. 給　　　（动）gěi　to give
6. 看　　　（动）kàn　to see, to look at
7. 来　　　（动）lái　to come
8. 有　　　（动）yǒu　to have
9. 没　　　（副）méi　not
10. 只　　　（副）zhǐ　only
11. 本子　　（名）běnzi [本] note-book

語法 Yǔfǎ Grammar

16.1 The Sentence with a Verbal Predicate   A sentence in which the predicate is composed of a verb is called the sentence with a verbal predicate. A verb is a word that describes some action, behaviour or change. In the sentence with a verbal predicate, the predicate tells about the action, behaviour or change of the person or thing denoted by the subject. The sentence with a verbal predicate may be divided into three kinds:

(1) The simple verbal sentence   This is the kind of sentence where there is only a verb and no object, that is to say, the predicate of such a sentence is formed by the verb itself. e. g.

1. 先生　工作.
   Xiānshēng gōngzuò.
   The teacher works.

2. 我們　学習.
   Wǒmen　xuéxí.
   We study.

(2) The verbal sentence with a single object   This is the kind of sentence where the predicate is made up of a verb and its object.   The verb precedes the object. e. g.

3. 先生　教　我.
   Xiānshēng jiāo　wǒ.
   The teacher teaches me.

4. 我們　学習　中文.
   Wǒmen　xuéxí　zhōngwén.
   We study Chinese.

先生 and 我們 are subjects, 教 and 学習 are verbs, and 我 and 中文 are objects.   The subject precedes the predicate.   The following word order is recognized as the basic construction of the verbal sentence:

Subject — Verb — Object

(3) The verbal sentence with double object   This is the kind of sentence where there may be one verb and two objects in the predicate.   Such a sentence is called the verbal sentence with double object.   The verb precedes the objects, and the indirect object (which in general denotes some person) precedes the direct object (which in general denotes some thing).e. g.

5. 先生　教　我　中文.
   Xiānshēng jiāo　wǒ　zhōngwén.
   The teacher teaches me Chinese.

6. 他　給　朋友　一枝　鉛笔.
   Tā　gěi　péngyǒu　yìzhī　qiānbǐ.

He gives his friend a (one) pencil.

先生 and 他 are subjects, 教 and 給 are verbs. 中文 and
鉛笔 are direct objects, while 我 and 朋友 are indirect objects.
Therefore, the word order of the verbal sentence with double
object is as follows:

Subject — Verb — Indirect Object — Direct Object

In example 6, the object (or the noun 鉛笔) is preceded by an
adjective modifier made up of a numeral and a measure word
一枝. In fact, all the subjects and objects in such sentences can
be preceded by adjective modifiers. In the following example,
the subject and the objects all have adjective modifiers:

7. 我們　先生　給　那个　学生　一本
   Wǒmén　xiānshêng　gěi　nèigê　xuéshêng　yìběn

   很　新的　書.
   hěn　xīndê　shū.

Our teacher gives that student a very new book.

**16.2 The Negative Form of the Sentence with a Verbal Pre-
dicate** Just like the negative forms of the sentence with a substantive predicate and the sentence with an adjectival predicate, we use the negative adverb 不 to form the negative of
the sentence with a verbal predicate. When we put the adverb
不 before the verb, it means "used not to do so", "shall or
will not do so" or "to be not willing to do so". e. g.

8. 我　不　看　这張　旧　报.
   Wǒ　bú　kàn　zhèizhāng　jiù　bào.

I do not read this old newspaper.

9. 我的　朋友　不　来.
   Wǒdê　péngyǒu　bù　lái.

My friend is not coming (OR: does not come).

10. 她　不　給　我　那張　紙.
    Tā　bù　gěi　wǒ　nèizhāng　zhǐ.

She is not giving me (OR: does not give me) that sheet
of paper.

16.3 **The Negative Form of** 有   The word 有 is a rather
special verb, its negative form is 沒有 and not 不有. e. g.

11. 我 <u>沒 有</u> 鉛笔.
Wǒ méi yǒu qiānbǐ.
I do not have a pencil.

12. 先生 <u>沒 有</u> 俄文 报.
Xiānshēng méi yǒu èwén bào.
The teacher does not have a Russian newspaper.

When there is some other element following 沒有, 沒有 can
be simplified as 沒 only. But at the end of a sentence, we
must say 沒有. e. g.

13. 你們 有 書 嗎?
Nǐmên yǒu shū mǎ?
Do you (plural) have books?

14. 他 有 書, 我 <u>沒</u> 書.
Tā yǒu shū, wǒ méi shū.
(or : 我 <u>沒 有</u>.)
Wǒ méi yǒu.
He has a book, I do not have a book (OR: I don't
have).

16.4 **How to Change a Sentence with a Verbal Predicate into
an Interrogative Sentence**   Such a sentence is changed into an
interrogative sentence either by adding the particle 嗎, or by
using the alternative form e. g.

15. 你 来 <u>嗎</u>?
Nǐ lái mǎ?
Are you coming?

16. 你 不 来 <u>嗎</u>?
Nǐ bù lái mǎ?
Aren't you coming?

17. 你 <u>来 不 来</u>?
Nǐ lái bù lái?
Are you coming (or not)?

When there is an object, this is the word order of the alternative interrogative sentence: the object may stand after the verbs or between the affirmative verb and the negative verb (refer to the alternative interrogative form of the sentence with a substantive predicate (1)). e. g.

18. 你們　学習　不　学習　俄文?
　　Nǐmên　xuéxí　bù　xuéxí　èwén?

Do you (plural) study Russian?

19. 你們　学習　俄文　不　学習?
　　Nǐmên　xuéxí　èwén　bù　xuéxí?

Do you (plural) study Russian?

20. 那个　同志　教　不　教　你們　中文?
　　Nèigê　tóngzhì　jiāo　bù　jiāo　nǐmên　zhōngwén?

Does that comrade teach you (plural) Chinese?

21. 那个　同志　教　你們　中文　不　教?
　　Nèigê　tóngzhì　jiāo　nǐmên　zhōngwén　bù　jiāo?

Does that comrade teach you (plural) Chinese (or not)?

If the verb is 有, we have to use the form 有没有 ... or the form 有 ...没有. e. g.

22. 他　有　沒　有　鉛笔?
　　Tā　yǒu　méi　yǒu　qiānbǐ?

Does he have a pencil?

23. 他　有　鉛笔　沒　有?
　　Tā　yǒu　qiānbǐ　méi　yǒu?

Does he have a pencil?

課文　Kèwén　Text
SIDE FOUR, BAND SEVEN

I

(a₁) 您　来　不　来?
　　Nín　lái　bù　lái?

Are you (formal) coming?

(b₁) 我　来，　您　来　吗？
　　　Wǒ　lái,　nín　lái　må?

Yes, are you (formal)?

(a₂) 我　不　来.
　　　Wǒ　bù　lái.

No.

II

(a₃) 他　看　俄文　書　吗？
　　　Tā　kàn　èwén　shū　må?

Does he read Russian books?

(b₃) 他　不　看，他　只　看　中文　書.
　　　Tā　bú　kàn,　tā　zhǐ　kàn　zhōngwén　shū.

No, he reads only Chinese books.

(a₄) 您　看　俄文　書　不　看？
　　　Nín　kàn　èwén　shū　bú　kàn?

Do you (formal) read Russian books?

(b₄) 我　看，我　学習　俄文，我　有　很
　　　Wǒ　kàn,　wǒ　xuéxí　èwén,　wǒ　yǒu　hěn
　　　多　俄文　書.
　　　duō　èwén　shū.

Yes; I am studying Russian and I have many Russian books.

III

(a₅) 这个　先生　教　不　教　你？
　　　Zhèigě　xiānshēng　jiāo　bù　jiāo　nǐ?

Is this teacher your instructor? (LIT.: This teacher teaches not teaches you?)

(b₅) 教　我，她　教　我們　中文.
　　　Jiāo　wǒ,　tā　jiāo　wǒmén　zhōngwén.

Yes, she is our Chinese instructor. (LIT.: Teaches me, she teaches us Chinese.)

(a₆) 她 教 俄文 不 教?
Tā jiāo èwén bù jiāo?
Does she teach Russian?

(b₆) 她 不 教 俄文, 只 教 中文.
Tā bù jiāo èwén, zhǐ jiāo zhōngwén.
She doesn't teach Russian, she teaches only Chinese.

(a₇) 她 教 他們 不 教?
Tā jiāo tāmén bù jiāo?
Is she their instructor? (LIT.: Does she teach them not teach?)

(b₇) 不 教, 她 只 教 新 学生.
Bù jiāo, tā zhǐ jiāo xīn xuéshēng.
No, she teaches only new students.

(a₈) 您的 朋友 有 本子 嗎?
Níndė péngyǒu yǒu běnzǐ mǎ?
Does your friend have a notebook?

(b₈) 有 本子, 他的 本子 很 多.
Yǒu běnzǐ, tādė běnzǐ hěn duō.
Yes, he has many notebooks.

(a₉) 那个 学生 有 本子 沒 有?
Nèigė xuéshēng yǒu běnzǐ méi yǒu?
Does that student have a notebook?

(b₉) 沒 有, 他 有 纸.
Méi yǒu, tā yǒu zhǐ.
No, he has paper.

課外練習 Kèwài liànxí Home Work

1) Copy all the new words in this lesson once.

2) Make sentences with each of the following verbs:

   (1) 工作   (2) 有   (3) 給

3) Copy the following sentences and underline the subjects,

the adjective modifiers, the verbs, and the direct objects and indirect objects:

For example:

那个 先生 教 我 中文.

(4) 这个 先生 来, 那个 先生 不 来.

(5) 您的 朋友 看 中文 报, 我的 朋友 看 俄文 报.

(6) 先生 給 学生 一本 新 書.

4) Answer the questions in the negative:

(7) 你 有 干淨的 紙 嗎?

(8) 那个 学生 看 俄文 書 不 看?

汉字表　Hànzì biǎo　Chinese Characters

1	工	一 丁 工
2	作	
3	習	羽 (丁 ㄱ 习 羽)
		白
4	教	耂 (土 耂 耂)
		攵
5	給	糸
		合
6	看	手 (ノ ニ 三 手)
		目 (丨 冂 冃 月 目)

7	来	一 一 一 三 平 平 来
8	有	一 ナ 有
9	没	シ シ シ 沙 没
10	只	
11	子	

Lesson 17

生詞 Shēngcí New Words

SIDE FIVE, BAND ONE

1.	鋼笔	(名) gāngbǐ	pen
2.	都	(副) dōu	all
3.	也	(副) yě	also, too
4.	桌子	(名) zhuōzi [張]	table
5.	和	(連) hé	and
6.	把	(量) bǎ	(a measure word)
7.	椅子	(名) yǐzi [把]	chair
8.	杂誌	(名) zázhì [本]	magazine
9.	画报	(名) huàbào [本]	pictorial
10.	北京大学	(名) Běijīngdàxué	Peking University
11.	会	(动) huì	to know how to do
12.	对了	duìle	yes, that is right
13.	有意思	yǒuyìsi	interesting

語法 Yǔfǎ Grammar

17.1 **The Sentence with a Substantive Predicate (2)** Nouns, pronouns and adjectives may all be used as adjective modifiers to modify nouns (15.1), therefore in the sentence with a substantive predicate (1), when the predicate is made up of a noun, it may carry any of these adjective modifiers. e. g.

1. 这本　書　是　<u>先生的</u>　書.

Zhèiběn　shū　shì　xiānshēngdě　shū.

This book is the teacher's book.

2. 那枝　鋼笔　是　<u>我的</u>　鋼笔.

Nèizhī　gāngbǐ　shì　wǒdě　gāngbǐ.

That (fountain) pen is my (fountain) pen.

3. 这个　本子　是　<u>新</u>　本子.

Zhèigě　běnzǐ　shì　xīn　běnzǐ.

This notebook is a new notebook.

We have already learned that the central word (or the word modified) may be omitted, if the context is clear without it (15.1), so all the above sentences may be recast as follows:

4. 这本　書　是　<u>先生的</u>.

Zhèiběn　shū　shì　xiānshēngdě.

This book is the teacher's.

5. 那枝　鋼笔　是　<u>我的</u>.

Nèizhī　gāngbǐ　shì　wǒdě.

That pen is mine.

6. 这个　本子　是　<u>新的</u>.

Zhèigě　běnzǐ　shì　xīndě.

This notebook is a new one.

Here, all the substantives used as central words (all of them being nouns: 書, 鋼笔, and 本子) have been omitted, but the noun, pronoun or adjective in the adjective modifiers may, together with the structural particle 的, assume the function of a substantive (先生的, 我的 or 新的). This is called the substantive construction. A sentence, in which the main element of the predicate is composed of such a substantive construction, is called the sentence with a substantive predicate (2).

With the exception of the chief element of the predicate which is composed of a substantive construction, the sentence with a substantive predicate (2) is essentially the same as the sentence with a substantive predicate (1). So far as the sentence structure is concerned, in the sentence of the second kind, the copula 是 is also required to connect the subject with the chief element of the predicate. As for its function, the predicate of the second kind is to explain the person or thing denoted by the subject. But speaking more in detail, the predicate of the second kind describes the quality of the person or thing denoted by the subject, or the kind of person or thing.

17.2 The Negative Form of the Sentence with a Substantive Predicate (2) We put the negative adverb 不 before the copula 是 to negate the sentence with a substantive predicate (1) as has been explained before. Here we do the same to negate the sentence with a substantive predicate (2). e. g.

7. 这本 書 是 先生的 嗎?
Zhèiběn shū shì xiānshêngdê mǎ?
Is this book the teacher's?

8. 这本 書 不 是 先生的.
Zhèiběn shū bú shì xiānshêngdê.
This book is not the teacher's.

9. 那張 紙 是 不 是 你的?
Nèizhāng zhǐ shì bú shì nídê?
Is that sheet of paper yours (or not)?

10. 不 是, 那張 紙 不 是 我的.
Bú shì, nèizhāng zhǐ bú shì wǒdê.
No, that sheet of paper is not mine.

11. 那个 本子 是 不 是 新的?
Nèigê běnzî shì bú shì xīndê?
Is that notebook a new one?

12. 不 是 新的.
Bú shì xīndê.
No (it is not a new one).

Note: The method of asking questions is the same as explained under the sentence with a substantive predicate (1).

17.3 都 and 也   We know that 不 is an adverb of negation, 很 is an adverb of degree and 只 is an adverb of extent.
Now, 都 is also an adverb of extent. As far as the meaning
is concerned, it refers to the persons and things that have
already appeared in the same sentence; its place in the syntax
is after the subject and before the predicate. e. g.

13. 先生　都　是　中国　人.
Xiānshêng dōu　shì Zhōngguó rén.
All the teachers are Chinese.

14. 她的　書　都　是　俄文的.
Tādê　shū　dōu　shì　èwéndê.
All her books are Russian ones.

Note: In Chinese, when a plural noun is used as subject,
the plural number is always expressed by the adverb 都.
Although example 13 may be changed into 先生們都是中国人,
yet it would be not idiomatic if we say 先生們是中国人. In
example 14, the plural number of 書 is of course expressed
by the adverb 都.

"也" is also an adverb, and like the adverb "都" it has
to be put before the predicate. e. g.

15. 这本　書　好,　那本　書　也　好.
Zhèibên　shū　hǎo,　nèibên　shū　yê　hǎo.
This book is good, that book is also good.

16. 我　看　报,　他　也　看　报.
Wô　kàn　bào,　tā　yê　kàn　bào.
I read newspapers, he also reads newspapers.

We must not say 也那本書 or 也他. Similarly, it is not
correct to say 都先生 and 都她的書.

In general, adverbs, especially when monosyllabic, are not
used as predicates, therefore they cannot be used to answer
questions by themselves (the negative adverb 不 is an exception), for they must be affixed to verbs or adjectives. 都 and
也 come under the same rule. e. g.

17. 你的　朋友　都　来　嗎?
Nǐdě　péngyǒu　dōu　lái　mǎ?
Are all your friends coming?

18. 都　来.
Dōu　lái.
Yes (they are all coming).

19. 黑板　很　干淨,　桌子　也　很　干淨　嗎?
Hēibǎn　hěn　gānjǐng,　zhuōzi　yě　hěn　gānjǐng　mǎ?
The blackboard is very clean; is the table very clean too?

20. 也　很　干淨.
Yě　hěn　gānjǐng.
Yes (it is very clean too).

When 都 and 也 are used together, the general rule is that 也 precedes 都. e. g.

21. 我們　是　学生, 他們　也　都　是　学生.
Wǒměn　shì　xuéshěng, tāměn　yě　dōu　shì　xuéshěng.
We are students, they are all students too.

17.4 和　The chief function of this conjunction is to connect nouns and pronouns. e. g.

22. 这本　書　和　那本　書　都　好.
Zhèiběn　shū　hé　nèiběn　shū　dōu　hǎo.
This book and that book are both good.

23. 她　和　那个　同志　都　是　我的　朋友.
Tā　hé　nèigě　tóngzhì　dōu　shì　wǒdě　péngyǒu.
She and that comrade are both my friends.

24. 我　和　他　都　不　是　先生.
Wǒ　hé　tā　dōu　bú　shì　xiānshěng.
He and I are both not teachers. (LIT.: I and he all not are teachers.)

But in Chinese, not all nouns and pronouns are connected by conjunctions, particularly when two nouns stand together. There, we often use a pause instead of a conjunction. e. g.

25. 这本 书、 那本 书 都 好.
    Zhèiběn shū、 nèiběn shū dōu hǎo.

    This book (and) that book are both good.

26. 先生、 学生 都 来.
    Xiānshēng、 xuéshēng dōu lái.

    The teachers (and) students are all coming.

課文　Kèwén　Text
SIDE FIVE, BAND ONE

I

(a₁) 这張 桌子 是 您的 吗?
     Zhèizhāng zhuōzi shì níndě må?

     Is this table yours (formal)?

(b₁) 不 是, 这張 桌子 是 我 朋友
     Bú shì, zhèizhāng zhuōzi shì wǒ péngyǒu-
     的.
     dě.

     No, this table is my friend's.

(a₂) 这把 椅子 是 您的 不 是?
     Zhèibǎ yǐzi shì níndě bú shì?

     Is this chair yours (formal)?

(b₂) 也 不 是, 这把 椅子 也 是
     Yě bú shì, zhèibǎ yǐzi yě shì
     她的.
     tādě.

     It's not mine, either; this chair is hers too.

(a₃)   她   这本   杂誌   和   这本   画报   都
       Tā zhèiběn zázhì hé zhèiběn huàbào dōu

是   新的   吗?
shì xīndě må?

Are this magazine of hers and this picture news magazine (both) new?

(b₃)   都   是   新的,   她的   杂誌、   画报   都
       Dōu shì xīndě, tādě zázhì、 huàbào dōu

是   新的.
shì xīndě.

Yes, her magazine and picture news magazine are (both) new.

(a₄)   那个   先生   和   那个   学生   都   是
       Nèigě xiānshěng hé nèigě xuéshěng dōu shì

北京   大学的   吗?
Běijīng Dàxuédě må?

Do that teacher and that student (both) belong to Peking University?

(b₄)   都   是   北京   大学的.
       Dōu shì Běijīng Dàxuédě.

Yes. (They both belong to Peking University.)

(a₅)   你们   也   都   是   北京   大学的   吗?
       Nǐměn yě dōu shì Běijīng Dàxuédě må?

Do you also belong to Peking University?

(b₅)   不   都   是,   我   是,   他   不   是.
       Bù dōu shì, wǒ shì, tā bú shì.

Not both of us; I do, but he doesn't.

II

(a₆) 这本　杂誌　是　中文的　吗？
　　　Zhèiběn zázhì shì zhōngwénde mǎ?

Is this magazine Chinese?

(b₆) 不　是　中文的，是　俄文的．
　　　Bú shì zhōngwénde, shì èwénde.

　　　我　不　会　中文．
　　　Wǒ bú huì zhōngwén.

No, it's Russian. I don't know Chinese.

(a₇) 那本　画报　也　是　俄文的　吗？
　　　Nèiběn huàbào yě shì èwénde mǎ?

Is that picture news magazine Russian too?

(b₇) 不　是　俄文的，是　中文的．
　　　Bú shì èwénde, shì zhōngwénde.

No, it's Chinese.

(a₈) 你　看　中文　画报　吗？
　　　Ní kàn zhōngwén huàbào mǎ?

Do you read Chinese picture news magazines?

(b₈) 对　了，我　看　中文　画报．
　　　Duì le, wǒ kàn zhōngwén huàbào.

That's right, I do.

(a₉) 你的　朋友　也　都看　中文　画报
　　　Níde péngyǒu yě. dōu kàn zhōngwén huàbào

　　　吗？
　　　mǎ?

Do your friends (all) read Chinese picture news magazines too?

(b₉) 他們 也 都 看 中文 画报.
Tāmén yě dōu kàn zhōngwén huàbào.

中文 画报 很 有意思.
Zhōngwén huàbào hěn yǒuyìsî.

Yes, they do too. Chinese picture news magazines are very interesting.

(a₁₀) 你們 只 看 中文 画报 嗎?
Nǐmén zhǐ kàn zhōngwén huàbào mǎ?

Do you read Chinese picture news magazines only?

(b₁₀) 不, 我們 也 看 俄文 画报.
Bù, wǒmén yě kàn èwén huàbào.

No, we read Russian picture news magazines too.

課外練習 Kèwài liànxí Home Work

1) Translate and answer the following questions:—
(1) Are all your books and magazines new?
(2) Do these three students belong to Peking University?
(3) Are this magazine and that pictorial yours?
(4) Does that new pencil belong to your friend or not?

2) Change the following phonetic spellings into Chinese characters and write down the answers:

(5) Xiānshéngdê huàbào yǒuyìsî méi yǒu?
(6) Zhèibǎ yǐzî shì bú shì jiùdê?
(7) Nǐméndê xiānshéng huì bú huì èwén?

汉字表   Hànzì biǎo   Chinese Characters

1	鋼	金	
		岡（门门门门冈冈冈岡岡）	
2	都	者（土尹者）	
		阝	
3	也		
4	桌	丨卜占桌	
5	和	禾（丿禾）	
		口	
6	把	扌	
		巴（フ𠃌𤴓巴）	
7	椅	木	
		奇	大
			可（一口可）
8	杂	九（丿九）	
		木	
9	誌	言	
		志	
10	画		
11	会	人	

		云 (一 二 云)
12	对	
13	了	⁷ 了
14	意	立
		曰
		心
15	思	田
		心

Lesson 18

語法復習　Yǔfǎ fùxí　Review

18.1 The Sentence with a Substantive Predicate (1) and the Sentence with a Substantive Predicate (2)　We have already learned the sentence with a substantive predicate (1) (13.1). The syntax of the sentence is as follows:

Subject——Copula——Substantive.

For example:

1. 他　是　先生.
   Tā　shì　xiānshēng.

   He is a teacher.

2. 这　是　报.
   Zhèi　shì　bào.

   This is a newspaper.

Examples 1 and 2 are all simple sentences with substantive predicate (1), for after each 是, there is only a simple substantive. We know that nouns may take adjective modifiers, such sentences are rather complicated. e. g.

3. 那个　中国　学生　是　新　学生.
   Nèigè　Zhōngguó　xuéshēng　shì　xīn　xuéshēng.

   That Chinese student is a new student.

4. 很多　中国　学生　是　我們的　好
Hěn duō Zhōngguó xuéshēng shì wǒmêndê hǎo

朋友.
péngyǒu.

(Very) many Chinese students are good friends of ours.

Since substantives include nouns, pronouns, numerals and measure words, it is beyond question that pronouns, numerals and measure words may be used after 是. When a demonstrative pronoun, a numeral and a measure word make up the chief element of the predicate of a sentence, the whole sentence will also appear more or less complicated. e. g.

5. 我的　書　是　这　一本,　你的　是
Wǒdê shū shì zhèi yìběn, nǐdê shì

那　一本.
nèi yìběn.

My book is this one, yours is that one.

In examples 3,4 and 5, the elements after 是 are word groups: the first two are made up of nouns and their adjective modifiers, and the last one is a combination of a pronoun, a numeral and a measure word. Such sentences are still sentences with substantive predicates (1). Therefore whether the substantive after 是 is a single word or a word group does not make it a different kind of sentence. So long as the sentence is in agreement with the word order given above, it is called the sentence with a substantive predicate (1). So far as the function of such kind of sentence is concerned, the predicate is used to describe the person or thing denoted by the subject.

We have also learned the sentence with a substantive predicate (2) (17.1). The word order of this kind of sentence is as follows:

Subject — Copula — Substantive Construction (a noun, pronoun or adjective + "的")

In the sentence with a substantive predicate (2), the noun, pronoun or adjective and 的 after the copula form a substantive construction or its equivalent describing the quality of the

person or thing denoted by the subject, or the kind of the
person or thing. e. g.

6. 他的　　杂誌　是　　中文的.
　　Tādê　　zázhì　shì　　zhōngwéndê.

　　His magazine is a Chinese one.

7. 那本　　新　書　是　　他的.
　　Nèiběn　xīn　shū　shì　　tādê.

　　That new book is his.

8. 這張　　紙　是　　干淨的.
　　Zhèizhāng　zhǐ　shì　　gānjǐngdê.

　　This sheet of paper is a clean one.

Two points have to be noticed, when we use the sentence
with a substantive predicate:

(1) In the predicate, the copula has to be used. We cannot say 我学生 or 這張桌子干淨的.

(2) In the sentence with a substantive predicate (2), we
should use ...是...的 and the word 的 should never be omitted. We must say 這本杂誌是旧的, and we never say 這本杂
誌是旧.

18.2 The Sentence with an Adjectival Predicate and the Sentence with a Substantive Predicate (2)　　We have already
learned the sentence with an adjectival predicate (14.3), let
us look at the following examples:

9. 这个　　黑板　很　　大.
　　Zhèigê　hēibǎn　hěn　dà.

　　This blackboard is very big.

10. 这个　　黑板　很　干淨.
　　Zhèigê　hēibǎn　hěn　gānjǐng.

　　This blackboard is very clean.

The predicates of the above examples, 大 and 干淨, are made
up of adjectives. Such sentences are called sentences with
adjectival predicates, because the predicates are made up of
adjectives. Now let us look at more examples:

11. 这个　黑板　是　大的.
Zhèige　hēibǎn　shì　dàde.
This blackboard is a big one.

12. 这个　黑板　是　干淨的.
Zhèige　hēibǎn　shì　gānjìngde.
This blackboard is a clean one.

Although the words 大 and 干淨 are adjectives, with the use of 的, they have become substantive constructions. Therefore, the two sentences given above are sentences with substantive predicates (2).

There are marked differences between the sentence with an adjectival predicate and the sentence with a substantive predicate (2):

(1) The copula 是 can never be used before the predicate in the sentence with an adjectival predicate (14.3), should always be used in the predicate of the sentence with a substantive predicate (13.1, 17.1, 18.1).

(2) The adjective in the sentence with an adjectival predicate is descriptive in function; while in the sentence with a substantive predicate, the adjective with 的 is a substantive construction, which in conjunction with the copula, becomes a complete predicate, assuming the function of judgement or explanation.

According to the above, the sentence with an adjectival predicate is used for the purpose of description. When we wish to describe something or tell what it is like, we use the sentence with an adjectival predicate. When we ask "how is this blackboard" (这个黑板怎么样), we may answer:

13. 这个　黑板　很　大.
Zhèige　hēibǎn　hěn　dà.
This blackboard is very big.

14. 这个　黑板　不　大.
Zhèige　hēibǎn　bú　dà.
This blackboard is not big.

Or we may use other adjectives, such as 新, 旧, 長, 短, 小 and so on to describe the quality or shape of the blackboard.

On the other hand, the sentence with a substantive predicate (2) is used to judge of or explain something. When we ask "what blackboard" (什么黑板), "whose blackboard" (誰的黑板), "what kind of blackboard" (哪种黑板), "of what shape is the blackboard" (什么样的黑板) and so forth, then we have to use the sentence with a substantive predicate (2) in our answers.

Therefore, we may reach the conclusion that whenever we wish to describe the person or thing denoted by the subject, we use the sentence with an adjectival predicate, and whenever we wish to tell the kind of person or thing denoted by the subject, we use the sentence with a substantive predicate (2).

課文   Kèwén Text

I

SIDE FIVE, BAND TWO

(a₁) 先生、 学生 都 有 画报 吗?
Xiānshēng、 xuéshēng dōu yǒu huàbào må?

Do the teacher and the student (both) have picture news magazines?

(b₁) 不, 学生 有 画报, 先生 没 有
Bù, xuéshēng yǒu huàbào, xiānshēng méi yǒu

画报. 先生 只 有 杂誌.
huàbào. Xiānshēng zhǐ yǒu zázhì.

No, the student has a picture news magazine, but the teacher doesn't. The teacher only has a magazine.

(a₂) 画报、 杂誌 都 是 新的 吗?
Huàbào、 zázhì dōu shì xīndě må?

Are the picture news magazine and the magazine new ones?

(b₂) 是, 画报、 杂誌 都 是 新的.
Shì, huàbào、 zázhì dōu shì xīndě.

Yes, they are.

II

(a₃) 这 是 不 是 鉛笔?
Zhèi shì bú shì qiānbǐ?

Is this a pencil?

(b₃) 这 是 鉛笔.
Zhèi shì qiānbǐ.

Yes.

(a₄) 那 也 是 鉛笔 嗎?
Nèi yě shì qiānbǐ må?

Is that a pencil too?

(b₄) 对 了, 那 也 是 鉛笔.
Duì lê, nèi yě shì qiānbǐ.

That's right, it is.

(a₅) 这枝 鉛笔 和 那枝 鉛笔 都 是
Zhèizhī qiānbǐ hé nèizhī qiānbǐ dōu shì

你的 嗎?
nǐdê må?

Are this pencil and that one yours?

(b₅) 不, 短的 是 我的, 長的 是 我
Bù, duǎndê shì wǒdê, chángdê shì wǒ

朋友的.
péngyôudê.

No, the short one is mine and the long one is my friend's.

III

(a₆) 您 工作 不 工作?
Nín gōngzuò bù gōngzuò?

Do you (formal) work (not work)?

(b₆)   不 工作, 我 学习. 您 也 学习 吗?
Bù gōngzuò, wǒ xuéxí. Nín yě xuéxí ma?
No, I study. Do you study too?

(a₇)   我 不 学习, 我 工作. 我 教 中文.
Wǒ bù xuéxí, wǒ gōngzuò. Wǒ jiāo zhōngwén.
No, I work. I teach Chinese.

(b₇)   您的 学生 多 不 多?
Níndě xuéshěng duō bù duō?
Do you (formal) have many students?

(a₈)   我的 学生 不 少.
Wǒdě xuéshěng bù shǎo.
I have not a few students. (LIT.: My students are not few.)

(b₈)   您 教 俄文 不 教?
Nín jiāo èwén bù jiāo?
Do you teach Russian?

(a₉)   不 教, 我 不 会 俄文.
Bù jiāo, wǒ bú huì èwén.
No, I don't know Russian.

IV

(a₁₀)   你 有 本子 没 有?
Nǐ yǒu běnzǐ méi yǒu?
Do you have a notebook?

(b₁₀)   没 有, 我 有 纸, 没 有 本子.
Méi yǒu, wǒ yǒu zhǐ, méi yǒu běnzǐ.
No, I have paper; I do not have a notebook.

(a₁₁)   他 有 本子 没 有?
Tā yǒu běnzǐ méi yǒu?
Does he have a notebook?

(b₁₁) 他 有 本子, 也 有 紙.
Tā yǒu běnzǐ, yě yǒu zhǐ.

He has a notebook and paper too.

(a₁₂) 这張 紙 是 干淨的 不 是?
Zhèizhāng zhǐ shì gānjìngdè bú shì?

Is this sheet of paper a clean one?

(b₁₂) 是 干淨的, 这張 紙 很 干淨.
Shì gānjìngdè, zhèizhāng zhǐ hěn gānjìng.

Yes, this sheet of paper is (very) clean.

Lesson 19

生詞 Shēngcí New Words
SIDE FIVE, BAND THREE

1.	誰	(代)	shéi	who
2.	什么	(代)	shénmò	what
3.	哪	(代)	něi	which
4.	怎么样	(代)	zěnmòyàng	how (is it)
5.	叫	(动)	jiào	to call, to be called
6.	名字	(名)	míngzì	name
7.	些	(量)	xiē	some
8.	懂	(动)	dǒng	to understand
9.	学	(动)	xué	to learn, to study
10.	国	(名)	guó	country
11.	苏联	(名)	Sūlián	the Soviet Union
12.	知道	(动)	zhīdǎo	to know
13.	人民	(名)	rénmín	people
14.	同屋	(名)	tóngwū	roommate

語法 Yǔfǎ Grammar

19.1 **The Interrogative Sentence (3)** In the previous lessons, we have learned two kinds of interrogative sentences (13.3, 15.3). Here, we will deal with the third kind of interrogative sentence, made by using interrogative pronouns. e. g.

1. 他　是　誰?
   Tā　shì　shéi?

   Who is he? (LIT.: He is who?)

2. 他　是　先生.
   Tā　shì　xiānshēng.

   He is a teacher.

3. 这　是　什么?
   Zhèi　shì　shénmó?

   What is this? (LIT.: This is what?)

4. 这　是　画报.
   Zhèi　shì　huàbào.

   This is a picture news magazine.

5. 哪枝　鉛笔　短?
   Něizhī　qiānbǐ　duǎn?

   Which pencil is short?

6. 这枝　鉛笔　短.
   Zhèizhī　qiānbǐ　duǎn.

   This pencil is short.

7. 那本　杂誌　怎么样?
   Nèiběn　zázhì　zěnmóyàng?

   How is that magazine?

8. 那本　杂誌　很　好.
   Nèiběn　zázhì　hěn　hǎo.

   That magazine is very good.

In the above, 誰, 什么, 哪, and 怎么样, are all interrogative pronouns.

There are two points to be noticed, when we use this kind of interrogative sentence:

(1) The question is asked by using the interrogative pronoun in the sentence, so the interrogative pronoun has to be placed where an answer is expected. e. g.

9. 誰　教　你們　中文?
Shéi　jiāo　nǐmen　zhōngwén?
Who teaches you (plural) Chinese?

10. 那个　先生　教　我們　中文.
Nèige　xiānshěng　jiāo　wǒmen　zhōngwén.
That teacher teaches us Chinese.

11. 他　教　誰　中文?
Tā　jiāo　shéi　zhōngwén?
Whom does he teach Chinese?

12. 他　教　我們　中文.
Tā　jiāo　wǒmen　zhōngwén.
He teaches us Chinese.

The questions appear in different places in the above two examples, and the same word 誰 is used in two different positions; in the first sentence, it is used as subject, and in the second, it is used as object. Other examples are:

13. 你　看　哪本　画报?
Nǐ　kàn　něiběn　huàbào?
Which picture news magazine do you read?

14. 我　看　这本　画报.
Wǒ　kàn　zhèiběn　huàbào.
I read this picture news magazine.

15. 哪本　画报　有意思?
Něiběn　huàbào　yǒuyìsi?
Which picture news magazine is interesting?

16. 这本　画报　有意思.
Zhèiběn　huàbào　yǒuyìsi.
This picture news magazine is interesting.

For the same reasons, the same word 哪 is used as adjective modifier of the object and then as adjective modifier of the subject.

(2) The interrogative word itself forms an interrogative sentence; so there is no need to put the word 嗎 at the end of the sentence in which an interrogative pronoun has already been used.

19.2 The Substantive Sentence with the Verb 叫 There is one kind of sentence in which the verb of the predicate is 叫. The predicate of such kind of sentence is used mainly to tell the name of the person or thing denoted by the subject. e. g.

17. 这 叫 什么?
    Zhèi jiào shénmó?
    What is this called?

18. 这 叫 椅子.
    Zhèi jiào yǐzi.
    This is called a chair.

19. 他 叫 什么 名字?
    Tā jiào shénmó míngzì?
    What is his name? (LIT.: He is called what name?)

20. 他 叫 張友文.
    Tā jiào Zhāngyǒuwén.
    He is called Chāng Yǒu-wén.

This kind of sentence is also called the sentence with a substantive predicate. Here the verb 叫 is a special verb, the same in nature and function as the copula 是. Hence, the element following 叫 is not an object, but a substantive predicate.

Note: 什么 in example 19 is used as adjective modifier, and different in use from 什么 in example 17. It is very common to use it as an adjective modifier.

19.3 一些 些 is a measure word used to express some quantity or number. e. g.

21. 我 有 一些 杂誌.
    Wǒ yǒu yìxiē zázhì.

    I have some magazines.

22. 他　懂　一些　中文.
　　Tā　dǒng　yìxiē　zhōngwén.

He understands some Chinese.

The nouns following 一些 may be nouns denoting countable things (such as 杂誌), or nouns denoting uncountable things (such as 中文).

Except when used at the beginning of a sentence, 一 of 一些 may be omitted. e. g.

23. 他　有　(一)些　中国　朋友.
　　Tā　yǒu　(yì)xiē　Zhōngguó　péngyǒu.

He has some Chinese friends.

24. 先生　給　我　(一)些　杂誌.
　　Xiānsheng　gěi　wǒ　(yì)xiē　zázhì.

The teacher gives me some magazines.

When it is used together with 这, 那 and 哪, 一 is always omitted. Indeed we may say 这些, 那些, and 哪些 are the plural forms of 这, 那 and 哪. e. g.

25. 这些　鉛笔　都　是　短的.
　　Zhèixiē　qiānbǐ　dōu　shì　duǎnde.

These pencils are all short ones.

26. 哪些　桌子　干淨?
　　Něixiē　zhuōzi　gānjing?

Which tables are clean?

27. 那些　桌子　干淨.
　　Nèixiē　zhuōzi　gānjing.

Those tables are clean.

課文 Kèwén Text

SIDE FIVE, BAND THREE

I

(a₁) 那个 同志 是 誰?
Nèigè tóngzhì shì shéi?

Who is that comrade?

(b₁) 她 是 我的 朋友.
Tā shì wǒdè péngyǒu.

She is my friend.

(a₂) 哪个 先生 教 她?
Něigè xiānshēng jiāo tā?

Which teacher is her instructor?

(b₂) 張 先生 教 她.
Zhāng xiānshēng jiāo tā.

Her instructor is Mr. Chang.

(a₃) 她 学 什么?
Tā xué shénmò?

What does she study?

(b₃) 她 学 中文.
Tā xué zhōngwén.

She studies Chinese.

(a₄) 她 是 哪国 人?
Tā shì něiguó rén?

Where is she from?

(b₄) 她 是 苏联 人.
Tā shì Sūlián rén.

She is from the Soviet Union.

(a₅) 她　叫　什么　名字?
Tā　jiào　shénmô　míngzî?
What is her name?

(b₅) 我　不　知道.
Wǒ　bù　zhīdào.
I don't know.

(a₆) 她的　中文　怎么样?
Tādê　zhōngwén　zěnmôyàng?
How is her Chinese?

(b₆) 不　很　好,　懂　一些.
Bù　hěn　hǎo,　dǒng　yìxiē.
Not very good; she understands a little.

II

(a₇) 这本　书　是　誰的?
Zhèiběn　shū　shì　shéidê?
Whose book is this?

(b₇) 这本　书　是　我的.
Zhèiběn　shū　shì　wǒdê.
This book is mine.

(a₈) 这　是　一本　什么　书?
Zhèi　shì　yìběn　shénmô　shū?
What kind of book is this?

(b₈) 这　是　一本　中文　书.
Zhèi　shì　yìběn　zhōngwén　shū.
This is a Chinese book.

(a₉) 这 叫 什么?
Zhèi jiào shénmǒ?
What is this called?

(b₉) 这 叫 画报.
Zhèi jiào huàbào.
This is called a picture news magazine.

(a₁₀) 这 是 什么 画报?
Zhèi shì shénmǒ huàbào?
What picture news magazine is this?

(b₁₀) 这 是 "人民 画报".
Zhèi shì "Rénmín Huàbào".
This is "The People's Picture Magazine."

(a₁₁) "人民 画报" 怎么样?
"Rénmín Huàbào" zěnmǒyàng?
How is "The People's Picture Magazine?"

(b₁₁) 很 有意思.
Hěn yǒuyìsi.
Very interesting.

(a₁₂) 那些 是 什么?
Nèixiē shì shénmǒ?
What are those?

(b₁₂) 哪些? 这些 都 是 旧 杂誌.
Něixiē? Zhèixiē dōu shì jiù zázhì.
Which ones? These are all old magazines.

(a₁₃) 那些 旧 杂誌 都 怎么样?
Nèixiē jiù zázhì dōu zěnmǒyàng?
How are those old magazines?

(b₁₃) 我   也   不   知道.   这些   杂誌   都
     Wǒ   yě   bù   zhīdào. Zhèixiē zázhì   dōu

不   是   我的.   都   是   我   同屋
bú   shì   wǒdê.   Dōu   shì   wǒ   tóngwū-

的.
dê.

I don't know myself. These magazines aren't mine.
They are my roommate's.

課外練習   Kèwài liànxí   Home Work

1)   Answer the following questions (Names of persons and coun-
tries may be written in phonetic spellings.):

(1) 你的   同屋   叫   什么   名字?

(2) 你   知道   他的   中国   名字   吗?

(3) 这个   同志   是   哪国   人?

(4) 他   懂   不   懂   俄文?

2)   Make sentences with each of the following words and word
combinations:

(5) 誰的

(6) 哪些

(7) 什么

(8) 怎么样

汉字表 Hànzì biǎo Chinese Characters

1	誰		
2	什	亻	
		十	
3	么	丿	么
4	哪	口	
		那	
5	怎	乍	
		心	
6	样	木	
		羊（丶 丷 兰 羊）	
7	叫	口	
		丩（凵 丩）	
8	名	夕	
		口	
9	字		
10	些	丨 十 止 止 此 此 此 些	
11	懂	忄	
		董	艹
			重（丿 一 亠 宵 旨 軍 重）

12	苏	艹
		办（力 力 办）
13	联	耳
		关（丶 丷 䒑 兰 䒑 关）
14	知	
15	道	
16	民	乛 コ ア 尺 民
17	屋	尸
		至（一 云 至）

Lesson 20

生詞 Shēngcí New Words

SIDE FIVE, BAND FOUR

1. 积极　　　(形) jījí　　　enthusiastic, active
2, 努力　　　(形) nǔlì　　　diligent, strenuous
3. 跟　　　　(介) gēn　　　with, after
4. 从　　　　(介) cóng　　　from
5. 学校　　　(名) xuéxiào　school
6. 一起　　　(副) yìqǐ　　　together
7. 那兒(那里) (代) nàr (nàlǐ)　there
8. 这兒(这里) (代) zhèr(zhèlǐ) here
9. 去　　　　(动) qù　　　　to go
10. 地　　　　(助) dē　　　　(a structural particle)
11. 高兴　　　(形) gāoxìng　glad, happy
12. 喜欢　　　(动) xǐhuǎn　to like, to be fond of
13. 电影　　　(名) diànyǐng　film, moving picture
14. 哪兒(哪里) (代) nǎr (nǎlǐ)　where

語法 Yǔfǎ Grammar

20.1 The Adverbial Modifier   The adverbial modifier is an element used to modify the verb or the adjective. Besides adverbs, there are many words of other parts of speech and constructions that can function as adverbial modifiers. In this lesson, only adjectives and prepositional constructions are introduced as adverbial modifiers.

(1) Adjectives Used as Adverbial Modifiers   Adjectives are not only used as adjective modifiers and predicates, but also as adverbial modifiers. e. g.

1. 这个　同志　积极　工作.
Zhèige   tóngzhì   jījí   gōngzuò.
This comrade works enthusiastically.

2. 他的　同屋　努力　学習.
Tāde   tóngwū   nǔlì   xuéxí.
His roommate studies diligently.

Here, the adjectives 积极 and 努力 are used as adverbial modifiers to 工作 and 学習. Adverbial modifiers are always put before the central words or the words modified.

(2) The Prepositional Construction (Phrase) Used as Adverbial Modifier   A preposition always carries its own object in a prepositional construction. It can be used either as adjective modifier or as adverbial modifier. When it is used as adverbial modifier, it has to be placed before the central word. e. g.

3. 我　朋友　跟　我　很　好.
Wǒ   péngyǒu   gēn   wǒ   hěn   hǎo.
My friend is very good to me.

4. 那个　同志　从　学校　来.
Nèige   tóngzhì   cóng   xuéxiào   lái.
That comrade is coming (or: comes) from school.

跟 and 从 are prepositions, and 跟我 and 从学校 are prepositional constructions. 跟我 modifies the adjective 好, and 从学校 modifies the verb 来.

In Chinese, there are some prepositions that are rather difficult to use properly. For the present, let us discuss only the following two prepositions 跟 and 从:

(1) 跟 It is commonly used in two ways. It may be used with the meaning of "to" or "with," pointing out the object to which action or feeling is directed. See example 3. It may also be used with the meaning of "together with." e. g.

5. 她 跟 我 看 一張 报.
　　Tā gēn wǒ kàn yìzhāng bào.
She is reading a newspaper (together) with me. (LIT.: She with me reads one sheet newspaper.)

The adverb 一起 is often used together with the prepositional construction composed of 跟. e. g.

6. 我 朋友 跟 我 一起 学習.
　　Wǒ péngyǒu gēn wǒ yìqǐ xuéxí.
My friend studies (together) with me.

(2) 从 从 denotes a starting point, its object may be a word or word group of time or of place. 学校 in example 4 is a word denoting place. (The words expressing time will be introduced afterwards.) When such a construction is used to represent place, the object must be a noun or pronoun denoting place. e. g.

7. 先生 从 学校 来.
　　Xiānshěng cóng xuéxiào lái.
The teacher comes from school.

8. 他 从 那兒 来.
　　Tā cóng nàr lái.
He is coming from there.

When the starting point of an action is represented by a person or persons, we have to change the noun or pronoun denoting persons into a word for place by adding 这兒 or 那兒. e. g.

9. 他 从 朋友 那兒 来.
Tā cóng péngyǒu nàr lái.

He is coming from (seeing) his friend (OR: from his friend's place). (LIT.: He from friend there comes.)

10. 我 从 你 这兒 去.
Wǒ cóng nǐ zhèr qù.

I am going (away) from you. (LIT.: I from you here go.)

20.2 The Repetition of Adjectives In Chinese, adjectives can be repeated by reduplicating the syllable:

11. 好 ⟶ 好好兒
    hǎo ⟶ hǎohāor
    good   very good

12. 干净 ⟶ 干干净净
    gānjìng ⟶ gāngānjìngjìng
    clean   very clean

When a monosyllabic adjective is reduplicated, the second syllable is always pronounced in the 1st tone with the retroflex "兒". When a dissyllabic adjective is reduplicated, the final syllable is always stressed.

The reduplicated adjective has the function of emphasizing the quality expressed by that adjective. It can be used either as adjective modifier or as adverbial modifier. As adverbial modifier, it is in general followed by the structural particle 地 (also written as 的) to join it with the central word. e. g.

13. 我們 都 好好兒地 学習.
Wǒmén dōu hǎohāordè xuéxí.

We all study very well.

14. 同志們 都 高高兴兴地 工作.
Tóngzhìmén dōu gāogāoxìngxìngdè gōngzuò.

All the comrades work very gladly.

課文 Kèwén Text
SIDE FIVE, BAND FOUR

I

(a₁) 那个　新　同志　是　誰?
Nèigè　xīn　tóngzhì　shì　shéi?

Who is that new comrade?

(b₁) 那个　新　同志　是　我的　朋友.
Nèigè　xīn　tóngzhì　shì　wǒdè　péngyǒu.

他的　名字　叫　張友文.
Tādè　míngzì　jiào　Zhāngyǒuwén.

That new comrade is my friend. His name is Chāng Yǒu-wén.

(a₂) 那个　新　同志　怎么样?
Nèigè　xīn　tóngzhì　zěnmòyàng?

How is that new comrade?

(b₂) 很　好,　很　积極. 他　会　中文,　也
Hěn　hǎo,　hěn　jījí.　Tā　huì　zhōngwén,　yě

懂　俄文. 他　积極地　工作,　我們
dǒng　èwén.　Tā　jījídè　gōngzuò,　wǒmèn

都　喜欢　他.
dōu　xǐhuàn　tā.

Very good, very enthusiastic. He knows Chinese and understands Russian too. He works enthusiastically and we all like him.

II

(a₃) 这个　学生　学　什么?
Zhèigè　xuéshēng　xué　shénmò?

What does this student study?

(b₃) 他　学　中文.
Tā　xué　zhōngwén.

He studies Chinese.

(a₄)　他　跟　你　一起　学習　嗎?
　　　Tā　gēn　nǐ　yìqǐ　xuéxí　må?

Does he study together with you?

(b₄)　对了,　我們　一起　学習,　我們　很
　　　Duìlê,　wǒmên　yìqǐ　xuéxí,　wǒmên　hĕn

努力地　学習,　我們　都　高高兴兴
nǔlìdê　xuéxí,　wǒmên　dōu　gāogåoxìngxìng-

地　学習.
dê　xuéxí.

That's right, we study together; we study very diligently; we both study very gladly.

III

(a₅)　您　看　电影　不　看?
　　　Nín　kàn　diànyǐng　bú　kàn?

Are you (formal) going to see the film?

(b₅)　看.
　　　Kàn.
Yes.

(a₆)　您　从　哪兒　去?
　　　Nín　cóng　nǎr　qù?

Where are you going from?

(b₆)　我　从　学校　去,　你　也　从　学校
　　　Wǒ　cóng　xuéxiào　qù,　nǐ　yĕ　cóng　xuéxiào

去　嗎?
qù　må?

I am going from school; are you going from school
too?

(a₇)　不,　我　从　朋友　那兒　去.
　　　Bù,　wǒ　cóng　péngyǒu　nàr　qù.

No, I'm going from my friend's place.

課外練習　Kèwài liànxí　Home Work

Translate the following English into Chinese:
1) Where have you come from?
   I have come from teacher Chang's place.
2) With whom do you study?
   I study with him.
3) What do you study together?
   We study Chinese and Russian together.
4) Will you see the film (or the moving picture)?
   Yes. we will.　It is very interesting.

汉字表　Hànzì biǎo　Chinese Characters

1	积	禾	
		只	
2	極	木	
		亟（一 丅 了 丆 亟 亟）	
3	努	奴	女
			又
		力	
4	力		
5	跟		
6	从	人	
		人	
7	校	木	
		交（丶 亠 六 方 交）	

8	起	走 (土 キ キ 走 走)
		已 (フ コ 已)
9	兒	
10	里	日 旦 甲 里
11	去	
12	地	土
		也
13	高	、 ᅩ 古 古 高 高
14	兴	、 ᄼ ᄽ 兴 兴
15	喜	士 吉 壴 壴 喜 喜
16	欢	又
		欠
17	电	日 电
18	影	景	日
			京
		彡 (ノ ク 彡)

Lesson 21

生詞 Shēngcí New Words

1.	念	(动)	niàn	to read
2.	得	(助)	dē	(a structural particle)
3.	早	(形)	zǎo	early
4.	快	(形)	kuài	quick, fast
5.	写	(动)	xiě	to write
6.	汉字	(名)	hànzì	Chinese character
7.	晚	(形)	wǎn	late
8.	慢	(形)	màn	slow
9.	常常	(副)	chángcháng	often
10.	说(話)	(动)	shuō (huà)	to speak
11.	話	(名)	huà	words, speech
12.	太	(副)	tài	too
13.	跳(舞)	(动)	tiào (wǔ)	to dance
14.	一定	(副)	yídìng	certainly
15.	唱(歌兒)	(动)	chàng (gēr)	to sing (song)
16.	歌兒	(名)	gēr	song

語法 Yǔfǎ Grammar

21.1 The Verb-Object Construction   The construction composed of a verb and an object is termed a verb-object construction. Today we shall learn a special kind of verb-object construction. It has two characteristic features:

(1) So far as its meaning is concerned, it represents a single idea equivalent to a verb without object in English. e.g.

1. 我　念　書.
   Wǒ　niàn　shū.

   I study. (LIT.: I read book.)

2. 先生　教　書.
   Xiānshēng jiāo　shū.

   The teacher teaches. (LIT.: Teacher teaches book.)

Structurally speaking, 念書 and 教書 are two verb-object constructions, they are equivalent to two simple verbs "to study" and "to teach" in English. Here 書 is the object, but it is so habitually used that it has already lost the concrete meaning of "book". Yet, in the above examples, the word 書 is necessary, because in Chinese we are not accustomed to say 我念 and 先生教. Without 書 the meaning of the sentence is incomplete.

(2) So far as its construction is concerned, it is a combination of a verb and its object. It is the same in use as the general verb-object constructions. We must never use another object after such a construction. If another object is required, the habitually used object has to be omitted. e. g.

3. 我　念　中文.
   Wǒ　niàn　zhōngwén.

   I read Chinese.

4. 先生　教　中文.
   Xiānshēng jiāo　zhōngwén.

   The teacher teaches Chinese.

Then, we can't say 念書中文 or 教書中文.

21.2 **The Complement of Degree**　A word or words placed after a verb or adjective to tell something more about the action of the verb or the quality of the adjective are called a complementary element, and the verb or adjective is called the central word. The adjective modifier or the adverbial modifier is placed before the central word, while the complementary element is placed after the central word. There are several kinds of complementary element, here let us take a look at the complement of degree. Whenever we wish to describe emphatically the degree or extent (or result) an action has reached, we use the complement of degree. The action is often already completed (or taken for granted that it is completed), or it is habitually frequent, or has gained a certain level or result. e. g.

5. 他　来得　早.
   Tā　láidé　zǎo.
   He arrives early.

6. 我　念得　快.
   Wǒ　niàndé　kuài.
   I read quickly.

早 is used to complete 来, and 快 is used to complete 念.

21.3 Rules Concerning the Complement of Degree

(1) The main feature of the complement of degree is that between the verb and the complement there is a structural particle 得 used as connective. (得 and 的 have the same pronunciation, may be used interchangeably.)

(2) The complement of degree is generally composed of an adjective. But in a complicated sentence, it is very common to use a complicated construction as the complement of degree.

(3) If there is an object after the verb, we have to reduplicate the verb and place the complement after the second form of the verb. e. g.

7. 他　学　中文　学得　快.
   Tā　xué zhōngwén　xuédé　kuài.
   He learns Chinese quickly. (= As for learning Chinese, he learns it quickly.)

8. 先生 教 中文 教得 好.
Xiānshēng jiāo zhōngwén jiāodě hǎo.
The teacher teaches Chinese well.

Hence, in the special kind of verb-object constructions mentioned above, we have to reduplicate the verb too. e. g.

9. 他 念 書 念得 快.
Tā niàn shū niàndě kuài.
He studies quickly.

10. 先生 教 書 教得 好.
Xiānshēng jiāo shū jiāodě hǎo.
The teacher teaches well.

(4) In the sentence containing a complement of degree, the complement is very important. The verb or verbal construction standing before it seems merely the subject of the sentence. Therefore:

(a) In the negative sentence, the negative adverb 不 is not placed before the verb (or adjective) but before the complement. e. g.

11. 他 来得 不 早.
Tā láidě bù zǎo.
He does not come early.

12. 我 写 汉字 写得 不 快.
Wǒ xiě hànzì xiědě bú kuài.
I don't write Chinese characters quickly. (= As for writing Chinese characters, I don't write them quickly.)

We do not often use a word in the negative form as complement; instead, we use its antonym. e. g.

13. 他 来得 晚.
Tā láidě wǎn.
He comes late.

14. 我　写　汉字　写得　慢.
Wǒ　xiě　hànzì　xiědê　màn.
I write Chinese characters slowly.

(b) In the alternative interrogative sentence, we give both the affirmative and the negative forms of the complement but not those of the verb. e. g.

15. 他　来得　<u>晚　不　晚</u>?
Tā　láidê　wǎn　bù　wǎn?
Does he come late?

16. 他　学　中文　学得　<u>快　不　快</u>?
Tā　xué　zhōngwén　xuédê　kuài　bú　kuài?
Does he learn Chinese quickly?

課文　Kèwén　Text

SIDE FIVE, BAND FIVE

I

1. 先生　　常常　来得　很　早.
Xiānshêng　chángcháng　láidê　hên　zǎo.
The teacher often comes very early.

2. 学生　也　来得　很　早.
Xuéshêng　yě　láidê　hên　zǎo.
The student also comes very early.

3. 先生　説　話　説得　不　太　快.
Xiānshêng　shuō　huà　shuōdê　bú　tài　kuài.
The teacher does not speak too quickly.

4. 那些　学生　跳　舞　跳得　很　高兴.
Nèixie　xuéshêng　tiào　wǔ　tiàodê　hên　gāoxìng.
Those students enjoy dancing very much.

5. 張　同志　看　中文　报　一定　看得
Zhāng tóngzhì kàn zhōngwén bào yídìng kàndẻ

很　快.
hěn kuài.

Comrade Chāng certainly reads Chinese newspapers very quickly.

6. 他　懂　俄文，　他　説　俄文　説得
Tā dǒng èwén, tā shuō èwén shuōdẻ

很　好.
hěn hǎo.

He understands Russian and speaks Russian well.

II

(a₁) 你們　学習得　怎么样?
Nǐmẻn xuéxídẻ zěnmỏyàng?

How do you study?

(b₁) 我　学習得　不　太　好，張　同志
Wǒ xuéxídẻ bú tài hǎo, Zhāng tóngzhì

学習得　很　好.
xuéxídẻ hěn hǎo.

I don't study too well, but Comrade Chāng studies well.

(a₂) 你們　写　汉字　嗎?
Nǐmẻn xiě hànzì mả?

Do you write Chinese characters?

(b₂) 写　汉字. 我們　都　写得　很　慢.
Xiě hànzì. Wǒmẻn dōu xiědẻ hěn màn.

Yes. We all write them very slowly.

(a₃) 張　同志　也　寫得　很　慢　嗎？
Zhāng tóngzhì yě xiědê hěn màn mâ?
Does Comrade Chāng also write them very slowly?

(b₃) 不，張　同志　寫得　很　快.
Bù, Zhāng tóngzhì xiědê hěn kuài.
No, Comrade Chāng writes them very quickly.

(a₄) 你們　喜欢　唱　歌兒　不　喜欢？
Nǐmên xǐhuǎn chàng gēr bù xǐhuǎn?
Do you like to sing?

(b₄) 喜欢. 我們　常常　跟　中国　朋友
Xǐhuǎn. Wǒmên chángcháng gēn Zhōngguó péngyôu

一起　唱　歌兒. 中国　朋友　教
yìqǐ chàng gēr. Zhōngguó péngyôu jiāo

我們　中国　歌兒. 我們　跟　中国
wǒmên Zhōngguó gēr. Wǒmên gēn Zhōngguó

朋友　一起　唱得　很　高兴.
péngyôu yìqǐ chàngdê hěn gāoxìng.

We do. We often sing together with Chinese friends.
Our Chinese friends teach us Chinese songs. We enjoy
singing together with our Chinese friends.

課外練習　Kèwài liànxí　Home Work

1) Translate the following into Chinese:
  (1) This comrade always comes very early.
  (2) The students in our school learn Russian very rapidly.
  (3) I read Chinese books very slowly.

2) Complete the following sentences with complements of degree:

(4) 她　跳　舞　＿＿＿＿＿＿＿＿＿＿＿．

(5) 那些　中国　学生　说　俄文　＿＿＿＿＿．

(6) 先生　写　我的　名字　＿＿＿＿＿＿
　　　＿＿＿＿＿＿＿＿＿＿＿＿＿＿＿＿．

(7) 努力的　学生　一定　学习　＿＿＿＿
　　　＿＿＿＿＿＿＿＿＿＿＿＿＿＿＿＿．

(8) 我的　同屋　唱　中国　歌兒　＿＿＿
　　　＿＿＿＿＿＿＿＿＿＿＿＿＿＿＿＿．

汉字表　Hànzì biǎo　Chinese Characters

1	念	今（人 亼 今）
		心
2	得	
3	早	日
		十
4	快	
5	写	冖（丶 冖）
		与（一 与 与）
6	汉	

7	晚	日（1 刀 日 日）	
		免（ノ ク ク 召 召 召 免 ）	
8	慢		
9	常	尚	出（ノ ｜ ｜ ｜ 丬 屮 ）
			口
		巾（1 冂 巾 ）	
10	説	言	
		兑（ヽ ゝ 台 兑 ）	
11	話	言	
		舌（ノ 一 千 舌 ）	
12	太	大 太	
13	跳	足	
		兆（ノ ）丿 ｊ 兆 兆 兆 ）	
14	舞	無（ノ ヒ ｨ 二 午 舞 無 無 無 ）	
		舛（ク ク 夕 夗 舛 ）	
15	定	宀	
		疋	
16	唱		
17	歌	哥	可
			可
		欠	

Lesson 22

生詞 Shēngcí New Words
SIDE FIVE, BAND SIX

1.	二	(数)	èr	two
2.	四	(数)	sì	four
3.	五	(数)	wǔ	five
4.	六	(数)	liù	six
5.	七	(数)	qī	seven
6.	八	(数)	bā	eight
7.	九	(数)	jiǔ	nine
8.	十	(数)	shí	ten
9.	两	(数)	liǎng	two
10.	几	(数)	jǐ	how many, several, a few
11.	多少	(数)	duōshǎo	how many, how much
12.	半	(数)	bàn	half
13.	年	(名)	nián	year
14.	練習	(名、动)	liànxí	exercise, to exercise, to practise

語法 Yǔfǎ Grammar

22.1 **The Enumeration of Cardinal Numerals from One to Ninety-nine** In Chinese, the decimal system is used for counting numbers. Besides the numerals 一, 二, 三, 四, 五, 六, 七, 八, 九 and 十, are the numerals 十一, 十二 etc. The numerals from 11 to 99 are formed by the following three methods:

(1) From eleven to nineteen the numerals are formed by addition. For example: 11 is 10 plus 1; 19 is 10 plus 9.

(2) 20, 30, 40, 50, 60, 70, 80, 90 are formed by multiplication. For example: 30 is 10 multiplied by 3, 50 is 10 multiplied by 5.

(3) The numerals between the tens are formed first by multiplication, then by addition. For example: 22 is two tens plus 2, 78 is seven tens plus 8.

22.2 二 and 两   In Chinese, the numerals 二 and 两 denote the same number "two", but they are different in use:

(1) Before measure words we prefer 两 to 二. e. g.

1. 两个　朋友
   liǎnggè　péngyǒu
   two friends

2. 两張　桌子
   liǎngzhāng　zhuōzǐ
   two tables

There are a few exceptions, such as 二斤糖 (two catties of sugar) and 二年 (two years). Yet, even in such cases, we may use 两 instead of 二.

(2) If 2 comes at the end of a big number, we have to use 二 and never 两. e. g.

3. 十二个　学生
   shièrgè　xuéshěng
   twelve students

4. 四十二把　椅子
   sìshièrbǎ　yǐzǐ
   forty-two chairs

(3) "20" is only read as 二十, never as 两十.

22.3 几 and 多少   In asking about numbers or figures we use 几 and 多少; however, they are not always used interchangeably:

(1) 多少 may be used to ask about any number, big or small; while 几 is often used for the numbers from one to nine. For example:

5. 你 有 几本 "人民 画报"?
　　Nǐ yǒu jǐběn "Rénmín Huàbào"?
How many (copies of) "The People's Picture Magazine" do you have? (up to nine)

6. 你 有 多少本 "人民 画报"?
　　Nǐ yǒu duōshǎoběn "Rénmín Huàbào"?
How many (copies of) "The People's Picture Magazine" do you have? (any number)

Both sentences are questions about the number of pictorials. When the number of pictorials is less than ten, it is example 5; when the number of pictorials is indefinite, it is example 6. 几 is often used before 十. e. g.

7. 你 有 几十本 杂誌?
　　Nǐ yǒu jǐshíběn zázhì?
How many magazines do you have? (multiples of ten)

8. 你 有 十几本 杂誌?
　　Nǐ yǒu shíjǐběn zázhì?
How many magazines do you have? (between eleven and nineteen)

The expected answers will be 20, 30...or 90 to example 7, and 11, 12...or 19 to example 8.

(2) 多少 can be directly connected with a noun, while 几 must be followed by a measure word. e. g.

9. 这个 学校 有 多少(个) 先生?
　　Zhèige xuéxiào yǒu duōshǎo(ge) xiānshēng?
How many teachers are there in this school? (LIT.: This school has how many teachers?)

10. 那个　同志　有　几本　杂誌?
Nèigè　tóngzhì　yǒu　jǐběn　zázhì?

How many magazines does that comrade have? (up to nine)

22.4 半　It is a numeral. Be careful of the position of this numeral when it is used together with a measure word:

(1) When there is no numeral used together with 半, it can be directly placed before the measure word like the general numerals. e. g.

11. 半張　紙
bànzhāng　zhǐ

half a sheet of paper

12. 半年
bànnián

half a year

(2) When the word 半 is used together with numerals, the integral numerals are put before the measure word, while the word 半 follows the measure word. e. g.

13. 兩張半　紙
liǎngzhāngbàn　zhǐ

two and a half sheets of paper

14. 兩年半
liǎngniánbàn

two and a half years

課文　Kèwén Text

SIDE FIVE, BAND SIX

I

(a₁) 你　有　画报　嗎?
Nǐ　yǒu　huàbào　ma?

Do you have a picture news magazine?

(b₁) 有， 我 有 中文 画报, 也 有
Yǒu, wǒ yǒu zhōngwén huàbào, yě yǒu

俄文 画报.
èwén huàbào.

Yes, I have a Chinese picture news magazine, and a Russian one also.

(a₂) 你 有 多少本 中文 画报?
Nǐ yǒu duōshǎoběn zhōngwén huàbào?

How many Chinese picture news magazines do you have?

(b₂) 我 有 十二本 中文 画报.
Wǒ yǒu shíèrběn zhōngwén huàbào.

I have twelve Chinese picture news magazines.

(a₃) 你 有 多少本 俄文 画报?
Nǐ yǒu duōshǎoběn èwén huàbào?

How many Russian picture news magazines do you have?

(b₃) 我的 俄文 画报 不 多, 只 有
Wǒdě èwén huàbào bù duō, zhǐ yǒu

三本.
sānběn.

I don't have many Russian picture news magazines, only three.

II

(a₄) 这个 学校 有 多少(个) 苏联
Zhèigě xuéxiào yǒu duōshǎo(gě) Sūlián

学生?
xuéshěng?

How many Soviet students are there in this school?

(b₄) 有 二十二个 苏联 学生.
Yǒu èrshíèrgě Sūlián xuéshěng.

There are twenty-two Soviet students.

(a₅) 他們 都 学 中文 嗎?
Tāmĕn dōu xué zhōngwén må?
Do they all study Chinese?

(b₅) 他們 都 学 中文.
Tāmĕn dōu xué zhōngwén.
Yes.

(a₆) 几个 先生 教 这些 学生?
Jǐgĕ xiānshĕng jiāo zhèixiē xuéshĕng?
How many teachers instruct these students?

(b₆) 两个 先生.
Liănggĕ xiānshĕng.
Two teachers.

(a₇) 一个 先生 教 多少 学生?
Yígĕ xiānshĕng jiāo duōshåo xuéshĕng?
How many students does one teacher instruct?

(b₇) 一个 先生 教 十一个 学生.
Yígĕ xiānshĕng jiāo shíyīgĕ xuéshĕng.
One teacher instructs eleven students.

III

(a₈) 你 有 几个 中国 朋友?
Nǐ yǒu jǐgĕ Zhōngguó péngyǒu?
How many Chinese friends do you have?

(b₈) 我 有 三个.
Wǒ yǒu sāngĕ.
I have three.

(a₉) 他們 唱 不 唱 苏联 歌兒?
Tāmĕn chàng bú chàng Sūlián gēr?
Do they sing Soviet songs?

(b₉)　唱,　他們　唱　苏联　歌兒.
Chàng,　tāmĕn　chàng　Sūlián　gēr.
Yes, they do.

(a₁₀)　他們　会　多少　苏联　歌兒?
Tāmĕn　huì　duōshăo　Sūlián　gēr?
How many Soviet songs do they know?

(b₁₀)　他們　会　很　多.
Tāmĕn　huì　hĕn　duō.
They know many.

(a₁₁)　你　会　中国　歌兒　嗎?
Nĭ　huì　Zhōngguó　gēr　må?
Do you know Chinese songs?

(b₁₁)　会,　我　只　会　两个.
Huì,　wŏ　zhĭ　huì　liănggè.
Yes, (but) I know only two.

(a₁₂)　誰　教　你　中国　歌兒?
Shéi　jiāo　nĭ　Zhōngguó gēr?
Who teaches you Chinese songs?

(b₁₂)　我的　中国　朋友.
Wŏdĕ　Zhōngguó péngyŏu.
My Chinese friends.

(a₁₃)　你　常常　練習　嗎?
Nĭ　chángcháng　liànxí　må?
Do you practice often?

(b₁₃)　我　常常　練習.
Wŏ　chángcháng　liànxí.
Yes.

課外練習　Kèwài liànxí　Home Work

1) Write out the following numbers in Chinese and phonetic spellings and give the tone-marks:

　　(1)　16　　　(2)　32　　　(3)　95　　　(4)　40
　　(5)　22　　　(6)　81　　　(7)　53　　　(8)　77

2) Copy the following sentences and change the numbers within parentheses into Chinese numerals:

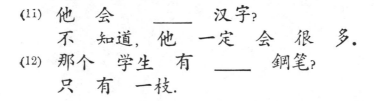

　(9)　那　(2)枝　短　鉛笔　是　誰的?

　(10)　他　有　(52)本　杂誌.

3) Fill the blanks with 几 or 多少 and pay attention to the use of the measure word:

　(11)　他　会　＿＿＿　汉字?
　　　　不　知道,　他　一定　会　很　多.

　(12)　那个　学生　有　＿＿＿　鋼笔?
　　　　只　有　一枝.

汉字表　Hànzì biǎo　Chinese Characters

1	二	一 二
2	四	丶 冂 冃 四 四
3	五	一 丁 五 五
4	六	丶 亠 六
5	七	一 七
6	八	
7	九	

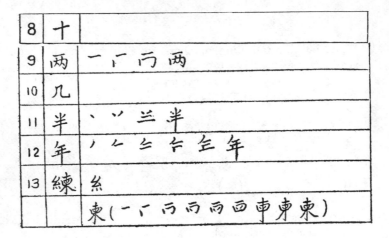

8	十	
9	两	一 厂 丙 两
10	几	
11	半	丶 丷 兰 半
12	年	丿 亻 仁 生 年
13	練	糸
		柬 (一 厂 丙 丙 丙 西 車 東 東)

Lesson 23

生詞 Shēngcí New Words

1.	在	(动) zài	to be on, in, at
2.	里边儿	(名) lǐbiānr	inside
3.	外边儿	(名) wàibiānr	outside
4.	上边儿	(名) shàngbiānr	above
5.	下边儿	(名) xiàbiānr	below, the following
6.	中間儿	(名) zhōngjiànr	middle
7.	前边儿	(名) qiánbiānr	front
8.	工厂	(名) gōngchǎng	factory
9.	后边儿	(名) hòubiānr	back, the following
10.	宿舍	(名) sùshè	dormitory, hostel
11.	作	(动) zuò	to do, to make, to work, to be
12.	地方	(名) dìfāng	place
13.	圖書館	(名) túshūguǎn	library
14.	礼堂	(名) lǐtáng	auditorium (hall)
15.	旁边儿	(名) pángbiānr	side, beside

語法 Yǔfǎ Grammar

23.1 在 在 is a verb and can be used as the chief element of a predicate. e. g.

1. 你 在 哪兒?

Nǐ zài nǎr?

Where are you? (LIT.: You are-at where?)

2. 我　在　学校.
　Wǒ　zài　xuéxiào.
　I am at school.

It can also be used as a preposition. If the object of 在 is composed of a word or word group of place, then this preposition and its object form a prepositional construction which is often used as adverbial modifier of place. e. g.

3. 我們　在　中国　学習,
　Wǒmên　zài　Zhōngguó　xuéxí.
　We are studying in China.

4. 先生　在　这兒　工作.
　Xiānshêng　zài　zhèr　gōngzuò.
　The teacher works here (LIT.: at here).

Whether the word 在 is used as a verb or a preposition, its object is in general a noun or pronoun denoting place. If the noun or pronoun denotes a person, then just as in the case of 从, 这兒 and 那兒 must be used to change this object into one denoting place. e. g.

5. 我的　練習　本子　在　先生　那兒.
　Wǒdê　liànxí　bênzî　zài　xiānshêng　nàr.
　My exercise notebook is at the teacher's place (LIT.: at teacher there).

6. 中国　朋友　在　我們　这兒　看　画报.
　Zhōngguó　péngyôu　zài　wǒmên　zhèr　kàn　huàbào.
　(Our) Chinese friend is reading a picture news magazine (here) at our place.

Of course, the word 在 may be followed by a noun denoting time.

23.2 Nouns of Locality　　Some nouns are used exclusively to indicate locality, e. g. 里边兒, 外边兒, 上边兒, 下边兒, 中間兒 etc. Like other nouns, a noun of locality can be used as subject. e. g.

7. 里边兒　很　干淨.
　Lǐbiånr　hěn　gānjìng.
　It is very clean inside. (LIT.: Inside very clean.)

It can be used as object. e. g.

8. 我　在　外边兒.
　Wǒ　zài　wàibiånr.
　I am outside.

It can also be used as adjective modifier. e. g.

9. 上边兒的　杂誌　是　新的.
　Shàngbiånrdě　zázhì　shì　xīndě.
　The magazine on top is a new one.

10. 我　不　看　下边兒的　旧　杂誌.
　Wǒ　bú　kàn　xiàbiånrdě　jiù　zázhì.
　I do not read the old magazine at the bottom.

As a central word, it can also be modified by a noun or a pronoun. e. g.

11. 那張　桌子　在　两把　椅子　中間兒.
　Nèizhāng zhuōzǐ zài liǎngbǎ yǐzǐ zhōngjiànr.
　That table is between the two chairs. (LIT.: That table is at the two chairs' middle.)

12. 先生　在　我們　前边兒.
　Xiānshěng zài wǒměn qiánbiånr.
　The teacher is in front of us.

In the word combinations of 两把椅子中間兒 and of 我們前边兒, the word 的 is often understood and omitted.

When 上边兒 and 里边兒 are used after nouns, we often omit the word 边兒. e. g.

13. 練習　本子　在　桌子上.
　Liànxí běnzǐ zài zhuōzǐshàng.
　The exercise notebook is on the table.

14. 我的　　同屋　　在　　学校里.
Wǒdě　　tóngwū　　zài　　xuéxiàolǐ.
My roommate is in the school.

In such cases, we may use the word 边兒 as well. But the other nouns of locality should not be shortened in this way, for their meanings will be different when 边兒 is omitted.

We have mentioned above that the particle 的 in such a word combination as 我們前边兒 may be omitted; but when 里边兒 and 上边兒 are already shortened into monosyllabic words 里 and 上, the particle 的 should not be used. That is to say: 桌子上 and 学校里 are correct, but not 桌子的上 and 学校的里.

23.3 **The Noun of Locality 里边兒**　　The noun of locality 里边兒 is rather peculiar in use. Some nouns require it, some don't, and still some others may or may not require it at all. The general rules are as follows:

(1) After geographical terms, we do not use 里边兒. e. g.

15. 我們　　在　　中国.
Wǒmên　　zài　　Zhōngguó.
We are in China.

16. 他的　　朋友　　在　　北京　　学習.
Tādě　　péngyǒu　　zài　　Běijīng　　xuéxí.
His friends study in Peking.

We must remember that in such cases, we never say 中国里边兒 or 北京里边兒.

(2) When the word 在 is followed by nouns such as names of buildings, organizations and so on, and if the meaning of 里边兒 is understood, then 里边兒 may or may not be omitted. e. g.

17. 他們　　都　　在　　工厂　　(里边兒)　　工作.
Tāmên　　dōu　　zài gōngchǎng　　(lǐbiǎnr)　　gōngzuò.
They all work in the factory.

If the persons are not inside the factory, we must use other nouns of locality, such as 外边兒 and 旁边兒 to indicate that they are outside or by the side of the factory etc. When there is no noun of locality following the object of 在, 里边兒 is understood as a rule.

(3) Some nouns, such as the nouns denoting implements, must take nouns of locality, because there are many sides of a thing and it is difficult to ascertain where without a noun of locality. Therefore 里边兒 cannot be omitted. e. g.

18. 那　半張　紙　在　書　里(边兒).
　　Nèi　bànzhāng　zhǐ　zài　shū　lǐ(biānr).

That half sheet of paper is inside the book.

We cannot omit the other nouns of locality.

課文　Kèwén　Text

SIDE FIVE, BAND SEVEN

I

1. 椅子　在　桌子　后边兒.
　　Yǐzi　zài　zhuōzi　hòubiānr.

The chair is in back of the table.

2. 桌子　在　椅子　前边兒.
　　Zhuōzi　zài　yǐzi　qiánbiānr.

The table is in front of the chair.

3. 人民　画报　在　杂誌　下边兒.
　　Rénmín　Huàbào　zài　zázhì　xiàbiānr.

"The People's Picture Magazine" is under the magazine.

4. 杂誌　在　画报　上边兒.
　　Zázhì　zài　huàbào　shàngbiānr.

The magazine is on top of the picture news magazine.

5. 我　同屋　在　宿舍(里)　唱　歌兒.
　　Wǒ　tóngwū　zài　sùshè(lǐ)　chàng　gēr.

My roommate is singing in the dormitory.

6. 他　朋友　在　書上　寫　名字.
　　Tā　péngyǒu　zài　shūshàng　xiě　míngzì.
　　His friend writes his name on the book.

7. 我　在　本子里　作　練習.
　　Wǒ　zài　běnzǐlǐ　zuò　liànxí.
　　I am doing exercises in my notebook.

8. 他　在　紙上　練習　汉字.
　　Tā　zài　zhǐshàng　liànxí　hànzì.
　　He is practicing Chinese characters on paper.

II

(a₁)　你們的　宿舍　在　哪兒?
　　　Nǐméndè　sùshè　zài　nǎr?
　　　Where is your dormitory?

(b₁)　在　北京　大学　里边兒.
　　　Zài　Běijīng　Dàxué　lǐbiānr.
　　　In Peking University.

(a₂)　你　在　什么　地方　学習?
　　　Nǐ　zài　shénmò　dìfāng　xuéxí?
　　　常常　在　宿舍(里)　学習　嗎?
　　　Chángcháng zài　sùshè(lǐ)　xuéxí　mà?
　　　Where (at what place) do you study? Do you study
　　　often in the dormitory?

(b₂)　我　在　圖書館(里)　学習.
　　　Wǒ　zài　túshūguǎn(lǐ)　xuéxí.
　　　我　同屋　在　宿舍(里)　学習.
　　　Wǒ　tóngwū　zài　sùshè(lǐ)　xuéxí.
　　　I study in the library. My roommate studies in the
　　　dormitory.

III

(a₃) 你們　圖書館　在　什么　地方?
Nǐmĕn　túshūguǎn　zài　shénmŏ　dìfāng?
Where is your library?

(b₃) 在　礼堂　旁边兒.
Zài　lǐtáng　pángbiānr.
Beside the auditorium.

(a₄) 你　在　圖書館(里)　都　作　什么?
Nǐ　zài　túshūguǎn(lǐ)　dōu　zuò　shénmŏ?
What do you do in the library?

(b₄) 念　書,　作　練習.　我　也　看　报.
Niàn　shū,　zuò　liànxí.　Wǒ　yě　kàn　bào.
圖書館的　报　很　多.
Túshūguǎndĕ　bào　hěn　duō.
I study and practice. I also read newspapers. There are many papers in the library.

(a₅) 这本　杂誌　也　是　圖書館的　嗎?
Zhèibĕn　zázhì　yĕ　shì　túshūguǎndĕ　mă?
Does this magazine belong to the library too?

(b₅) 不　是.　是　我的.　你　看,　这　是
Bú　shì.　Shì　wŏdĕ.　Nǐ　kàn,　zhèi　shì
我的　名字.
wŏdĕ　míngzi.
No. It's mine. Look, this is my name.

課外練習　Kèwài liànxí　Home Work

1) Make sentences with each of the following word combinations:

(1) 什么　地方
(2) 在...旁边兒

2) Translate the following into Chinese:

(3) The teachers' dormitories are outside the school, the students' dormitories are inside the school.

(4) The chairs in the front of the auditorium are new ones and those at the back are old ones.

3) Complete the following sentences according to the grammar rules given in this lesson:

(5) 学生　都　在　圖書館　＿＿.

(6) 我　同屋　在　張　同志　＿＿.

(7) 杂誌　在　書　上边兒,　画报　在　書　下边兒,　書　在　杂誌　和　画报　＿＿.

汉字表　Hànzì biǎo　Chinese Characters

1	在	一 ナ ナ 在
2	边	
3	外	
4	上	丨 卜 上
5	下	一 丁 下
6	間	門
		日
7	前	丷 (丶 丷 丷)
		月
		刂
8	厂	一 厂

9	后	ノ 厂 斤 后
10	宿	宀
		佰 亻
		百 (一 百)
11	舍	人 今 全 舍
12	方	
13	圖	门 冂 冃 冎 罔 悶 圄 圖 圖
14	館	食
		官 (宀 宁 宁 官 官 官)
15	礼	礻
		ㄴ
16	堂	尚
		土
17	旁	、 亠 亠 立 产 旁

Lesson 24

語法复習　Yǔfǎ fùxí　Review

24.1 The Adverbial Modifier and the Complement of Degree
We know that an adjective may be used as an adverbial
modifier before a verb or an adjective (20.1). It may also be used
as a complement of degree after a verb or an adjective (21.2).
As an adverbial modifier, the adjective is sometimes followed
by the structural particle 地 and sometimes not; but as a
complement of degree, it must be preceded by the structural
particle 得. Whether as an adverbial modifier or as a complement or degree, the adjective always says something about the
central word.　Hence it is necessary here to get a clear idea
of their different uses:

(1) It is very common to use an adjective as the complement of degree to a verb. In a sentence containing a complement of degree, the verb generally denotes a completed action
or an action that happens frequently. e. g.

1. 他　来得　很　早.
   Tā　láidě　hěn　zǎo.
   He (generally) comes early.

2. 他　学　中文　学得　很　快.
   Tā　xué　zhōngwén　xuédě　hěn　kuài.
   He learns Chinese very quickly.

Here 来 and 学 are two completed actions or actions that
have continued for some time, meaning "he comes early" or
"he is quick in learning". Here what we wish to express is not
"whether he has come or not" or "whether he is studying or
not"; because in such sentences, the actions of 来 and 学 have
already happened. Now what we wish to make clear is only

"how" have the actions proceeded. Therefore, a verbal sentence with a complement of degree possesses the nature of a descriptive sentence. And a sentence with an adjectival predicate followed by a complement of degree is of course a pure descriptive sentence.

(2) It is also common to use an adjective as adverbial modifier of a verb. In a sentence containing such an adverbial modifier, the action is not restricted by time, because in this kind of sentence the adverbial modifier is used to describe the way or manner of the action, and not to describe the extent or result of the action. Therefore, this kind of sentence with a verbal predicate is more narrative in nature.

24.2 The Use of the Structural Particle 地 after the Adverbial Modifier   The adverbial modifier is sometimes followed by the structural particle 地, and sometimes not. The following rules show when this particle 地 is needed:

(1) 地 should never be used under the following conditions:

a)   If the adverbial modifier is a monosyllabic word (it may be an adverb or an adjective), the particle 地 is not used. e.g.

3. 他　不　去.
    Tā   bú   qù.
    He is not going.

4. 我　一定　早　来.
    Wǒ   yídìng   zǎo   lái.
    I will surely come early.

b)   If the adverbial modifier is a prepositional construction, the particle 地 is not used. e. g.

5. 他們　从　礼堂　来.
    Tāmén   cóng   lǐtáng   lái.
    They are coming from the auditorium.

6. 我　跟　張　同志　跳　舞.
    Wǒ   gēn   Zhāng   tóngzhì   tiào   wǔ.
    I dance with Comrade Chāng.

(2) 地 is often not used.   If the adverbial modifier is a dissyllabic adverb, 地 is generally not used. e. g.

7. 我們　一起　学習.
　　Wǒmen　yìqǐ　xuéxí.

We study together.

There are a few dissyllabic adverbs that can be followed by the particle, but it is more idiomatic not to use it. e. g.

8. 他　常常（地）唱　歌兒.
　　Tā　chángcháng(dě) chàng　gēr.

He sings frequently. (OR: He often sings.)

(3) 地 is often used.　If the adverbial modifier is made up of a dissyllabic adjective or a reduplicated adjective, the particle 地 is more often used than not. e. g.

9. 他們　都　積極地　工作.
　　Tāmen　dōu　jījídě　gōngzuò.

They all work enthusiastically.

10. 我　一定　好好兒地　学習　中文.
　　Wǒ　yídìng　hǎohāordě　xuéxí　zhōngwén.

I will surely study Chinese well.

11. 朋友　都　高高兴兴地　唱　歌兒.
　　Péngyǒu dōu　gāogāoxìngxìngdě　chàng　gēr.

All the friends sing very gladly.

(4) 地 must be used.　In general, when an adjective used as an adverbial modifier is modified by another adverbial modifier, the particle must be used. e. g.

12. 他　很　努力地　学習.
　　Tā　hěn　nǔlìdě　xuéxí.

He studies very diligently.

課文　Kèwén　Text

SIDE SIX, BAND ONE

I

(a₁) 你　从　哪兒　来?
Nǐ　cóng　nǎr　lái?

Where are you coming from?

(b₁) 我　从　圖書館　来.
Wǒ　cóng　túshūguǎn　lái.

I'm coming from the library.

(a₂) 你　在　圖書館　作　什么?
Nǐ　zài　túshūguǎn　zuò　shénmǒ?

What do you do in the library?

(b₂) 学習　中文,　我　在　那兒　看　書,
Xuéxí　zhōngwén,　wǒ　zài　nàr　kàn　shū,

写　汉字,　作　練習.
xiě　hànzì,　zuò　liànxí.

I study Chinese; there I read, write characters and do my exercises.

(a₃) 你　不　看　电影　嗎?
Nǐ　bú　kàn　diànyǐng　mǎ?

Won't you see the film?

(b₃) 什么　电影?　是　苏联　电影　嗎?
Shénmǒ　diànyǐng?　Shì　Sūlián　diànyǐng　mǎ?

What film? Is it a Soviet film?

(a₄) 不　是，　是　中国的.　你　喜欢　不　喜
Bú　shì,　shì　Zhōngguóde.　Nǐ　xǐhuản　bù　xǐ-

欢　中国　电影?
huản　Zhōngguó　diànyǐng?

No, it's Chinese. Do you like Chinese films?

(b₄) 喜欢，　很　多　中国　电影　都　很
Xǐhuản,　hěn　duō　Zhōngguó　diànyǐng　dōu　hěn

好，　都　很　有意思.
hǎo,　dōu　hěn　yǒuyìsi.

I do, many Chinese films are (very) good and (very) interesting.

II

(a₅) 張　先生　在　哪兒?
Zhāng　xiānshēng　zài　nǎr?

Where is Mr. Chāng?

(b₅) 他　在　学生　宿舍(里).
Tā　zài　xuéshēng　sùshè(lǐ).

He is in the students' dormitory.

(a₆) 他　在　学生　宿舍(里)　作　什么?
Tā　zài　xuéshēng　sùshè(lǐ)　zuò　shénmo?

What is he doing in the students' dormitory?

(b₆) 他　在　那兒　跟　学生　說　話.
Tā　zài　nàr　gēn　xuéshēng　shuō　huà.

He is speaking with the students there.

(a₇) 他們　説　哪国　話?
Tāmén　shuō　něiguó　huà?

What language do they speak?

(b₇) 説　中国　話.　張　先生　是　中文
Shuō Zhōngguó huà. Zhāng xiānshěng shì zhōngwén

先生.　他　跟　学生　只　説　中文.
xiānshěng. Tā gēn xuéshēng zhǐ shuō zhōngwén.

Chinese. Mr. Chāng teaches Chinese. He speaks only
Chinese with the students.

(a₈) 学生　都　懂　嗎?
Xuéshēng dōu dǒng mǎ?

Do the students understand?

(b₈) 張　先生　説　中文,　学生　都　懂.
Zhāng xiānshěng shuō zhōngwén, xuéshēng dōu dǒng.

他　説　中文　説得　很　慢.　他
Tā shuō zhōngwén shuōdě hěn màn. Tā

常常　跟　学生　説　話,　学生　都
chángcháng gēn xuéshēng shuō huà, xuéshēng dōu

懂　他的　話.
dǒng tādě huà.

Mr. Chāng speaks Chinese; the students all understand. He speaks Chinese very slowly. He often
speaks with the students, and the students understand
what he says.

Lesson 25

生詞 Shēngcí New Words
SIDE SIX, BAND TWO

1.	月	(名) yuè	month
2.	今天	(名) jīntiǎn	today
3.	日	(名) rì	day
4.	号	(名) hào	day, number
5.	星期	(名) xīngqī	week
6.	天	(名) tiān	day
7.	点(鐘)	(名) diǎn(zhōng)	o'clock
8.	过	(动) guò	to pass, past
9.	分	(名) fēn	minute
10.	刻	(名) kè	a quarter
11.	差	(动) chà	less
12.	忙	(形) máng	busy
13.	今年	(名) jīnnián	this year
14.	现在	(名) xiànzài	now, at present
15.	时候兒	(名) shíhòur	time

語法 Yǔfǎ Grammar

25.1 Nouns of Time   In Chinese, some nouns are exclusively used to indicate time. So far as their functions are concerned, they are just the same as other nouns. They may all be used as subject, object, adjective modifier etc. in a sentence.

1. 一年 有 十二个 月.

Yìnián yǒu shíèrgè yuè。

There are twelve months in a year. (LIT.: One year has twelve months.)

2. 这 是 今天的 报.

Zhèi shì jīntiāndè bào。

This is today's paper.

一年 is subject, 十二个月 is object, and 今天 is the adjective modifier of 报.

25.2 The Expressions of Year, Month, Day and Hour In Chinese, indication of time begins from the biggest unit to the smallest unit, that is to say: 年 stands first, 月 second, 日 third, and then 时.

The year is always expressed in a simple way, e.g. "1957" is always read as 一九五七年, only very occasionally read as 一千九百五十七年 (one thousand nine hundred fifty seven). In a question, we use 哪 or 几, such as 哪年 or 一九五几年.

The designation of "months" in Chinese is very simple; the names of the twelve months in a year are formed by putting the numerals 1 — 12 before the word 月. Such as: 一月 (January) 二月 (February)... 十月 (October), 十一月 (November) and 十二月 (December). In a question, we say 几月.

The designation of "days" is also very simple. We have only to place the numerals 1 — 31 before 日 or 号. 日 is formal and often used in the written language, while 号 is always used in the spoken language. e. g. 二日 (号), 十日 (号) and 三十日 (号). In asking questions, we use 几号, 十几号, 二十几号.

In naming the seven days of the week, we place the numerals 1—6 after the word 星期. For example: 星期一 (Monday), 星期二 (Tuesday)... 星期五 (Friday) and 星期六 (Saturday); the seventh day in a week is called 星期日 (Sunday), it can also be shortened as 星期. In a question, we say 星期几.

Note: We can only say 一个月有三十天 (or 三十一天) and 一个星期有七天，but we cannot say 一个月有三十号 (or 三十一号)，and 一个星期有七号．

Time of the day is shown in the following:

3. 12:00   十二点（鐘）
shíèrdiǎn (zhōng)

4. 12:05   十二点　（过）　五分
shíèrdiǎn　(guò)　wǔfēn
(LIT.: twelve o'clock [past] five minutes)

5. 12:15   十二点　十五分
shíèrdiǎn　shíwǔfēn
十二点　一刻
shíèrdiǎn　yíkè
(LIT.: twelve o'clock one quarter)

6. 12:30   十二点　半（鐘）
shíèrdiǎn　bàn(zhōng)
(LIT.: twelve o'clock half)
十二点　三十分
shíèrdiǎn　sānshífēn

7. 12:45   十二点　三刻
shíèrdiǎn　sānkè
(LIT.: twelve o'clock three quarters)
十二点　四十五分
shíèrdiǎn　sìshíwǔfēn
差　一刻　一点
chà　yíkè　yìdiǎn
(LIT.: less one quarter one o'clock)

8. 12:55   十二点　五十五分
shíèrdiǎn　wǔshíwǔfēn
差　五分　一点
chà　wǔfēn　yìdiǎn
(LIT.: less five minutes one o'clock)

Therefore in a date, when the year, the month, the day and the hour are given at the same time, the word order is as follows:

9. 一九五七年 十月 一日（星期二） 十点
   yījiǔwǔqīnián shíyuè yírì (xīngqīèr) shídiǎn
   ten o'clock, (Tuesday), October 1, 1957 (LIT.: one-nine-five-seven-year ten-month one-day [week-two] ten-o'clock)

25.3 Words and Word Groups of Time Used as Adverbial Modifiers Words of time are not only used as subjects, objects and adjective modifiers, but also frequently as adverbial modifiers. When we wish to tell the time or period of a certain action, we use a word or word group of time as adverbial modifier. e. g.

10. 我　七点半　去.
    Wǒ qīdiǎnbàn qù.
    I am going at 7:30.

11. 他　星期二　很　忙.
    Tā xīngqīèr hěn máng.
    He is very busy on Tuesdays.

七点半 and 星期二 are both words of time. The adverbial modifier, 七点半, gives the time of 去, and 星期二 tells when he is busy. More examples are:

12. 我們　一天　学　十八个　汉字.
    Wǒmén yìtiān xué shíbágè hànzì.
    We learn eighteen Chinese characters in one day.

13. 我的　朋友　这个　月　很　忙.
    Wǒdě péngyǒu zhèigè yuè hěn máng.
    My friend is very busy this month.

一天 and 这个月 both represent certain periods of time. Here 天 indicates the time of the action 学汉字, and 这个月 tells when the state of 忙 (being busy) takes place.

When we wish to emphasize time, we may put the word or word group of time at the beginning of a sentence. e. g.

14. 星期二　他　很　忙.
    Xīngqīèr　tā　hěn　máng.

    On Tuesdays he is very busy.

15. 一天　我們　学　十八个　汉字.
    Yìtiān　wǒmén　xué　shíbágě　hànzì.

    In one day we learn eighteen Chinese characters.

25.4 有　有 is a verb, but it does not express any action. It shows a relation of ownership, and its subject is always a noun or pronoun denoting a person or persons. But if we wish to tell how many persons or things there are in a certain place, or how many smaller units there are in a definite period of time, we also use the verb 有. In such a case, the word or word group denoting place or time is the subject. e. g.

16. 一年　有　十二个　月.
    Yìnián　yǒu　shíèrgě　yuè.

    There are twelve months in a year. (LIT.: One year has twelve months.)

17. 北京　大学　有　很　多　学生,
    Běijīng　Dàxué　yǒu　hěn　duō　xuéshěng.

    There are many students in Peking University.

18. 圖書館里　有　很　多　書.
    Túshūguǎnlǐ　yǒu　hěn　duō　shū.

    There are many books in the library.

The above-mentioned sentences are by structure similar to the sentences 我有書 and 你有报. 一年，北京大学 and 圖書館里 are subjects. Therefore, it is idiomatic, especially in the spoken language, not to use the preposition 在 before the word or word group expressing place or time. We never say 在一年有十二个月 or 在北京大学有很多学生.

課文 Kèwén Text

SIDE SIX, BAND TWO

(a₁) 今年　是　一九六几年?
　　　Jīnnián　shì　yījiǔliùjǐnián?

What year is this (of the 1960's)?

(b₁) 今年　是　一九六一年.
　　　Jīnnián　shì　yījiǔliùyīnián.

This is 1961.

(a₂) 这个　月　是　几月?
　　　Zhèige　yuè　shì　jǐyuè?

What month is this?

(b₂) 这个　月　是　三月.
　　　Zhèige　yuè　shì　sānyuè.

This is March.

(a₃) 今天　是　几月　几号?
　　　Jīntiǎn　shì　jǐyuè　jǐhào?

What is the month and date today?

(b₃) 今天　是　三月　二十二号.
　　　Jīntiǎn　shì　sānyuè　èrshíèrhào.

Today is March twenty-second.

(a₄) 今天　是　星期几?
　　　Jīntiǎn　shì　xīngqījǐ?

What day of the week is today?

(b₄) 今天　是　星期三.
Jīntiǎn　shì　xīngqīsān.

Today is Wednesday.

(a₅) 一个　星期　有　几天?
Yíge　xīngqī　yǒu　jǐtiān?

How many days are there in a week?

(b₅) 一个　星期　有　七天.
Yíge　xīngqī　yǒu　qītiān.

There are seven days in a week.

(a₆) 这　七天的　名字　都　叫　什么?
Zhèi　qītiānde　míngzì　dōu　jiào　shénme?

What are the names of these seven days?

(b₆) 这　七天　叫:　星期一、　星期二、　星
Zhèi　qītiān　jiào:　xīngqīyī、　xīngqīèr、　xīng-

期三、　星期四、　星期五、　星期六、
qīsān、　xīngqīsì、　xīngqīwǔ、　xīngqīliù、

星期日.
xīngqīrì.

These seven days are called Monday, Tuesday, Wednesday, Thursday, Friday, Saturday and Sunday.

(a₇) 现在　是　几点　几分?
Xiànzài　shì　jǐdiǎn　jǐfēn?

What time is it? (LIT.: Now is how many hours how many minutes?)

(b₇) 现在　是　两点　过　一刻.
Xiànzài　shì　liǎngdiǎn　guò　yíkè.

It's a quarter after two. (LIT.: Now is two o'clock past a quarter.)

(a₈) 先生　什么　时候兒　来?
Xiānshêng shénmô　shíhôur　lái?
At what time is the teacher coming?

(b₈) 先生　两点半　来.
Xiānshêng liǎngdiǎnbàn　lái.
The teacher is coming at two-thirty.

(a₉) 这个　星期六　你　看　电影　吗?
Zhèigê　xīngqīliù　nǐ　kàn　diànyǐng　mâ?
Are you seeing a film this Saturday?

(b₉) 看,　这个　星期六　我　看　电影.
Kàn,　zhèigê　xīngqīliù　wǒ　kàn　diànyǐng.
Yes, this Saturday I'm seeing a film.

課外練習　Kèwài liànxí Home Work

1) Put the following units of time into Chinese:

(1) 7:05 (2) 4:50 (3) 8:30 (4) 11:00
(5) May first (1st of May) — Wednesday
(6) 8th of March 1958

2) Write out appropriate questions for the following sentences:

(7) 今天　是　星期五.

(8) 现在　是　十二点　过　十分.

(9) 一个　星期　有　七天.

(10) 我的　朋友　四月　三号　来.

3) Answer the following questions:

(11) 你　星期日　学习　不　学习?

(12) 这个　星期　你　哪天　忙,　哪天
不　忙?

汉字表　Hànzì biǎo Chinese Characters

1	月		
2	今		
3	天	一天	
4	日		
5	号	口 므 号	
6	星	日	
		生	
7	期	其(一 十 卄 井 甘 甘 其 其)	
		月	
8	点	占	
		⺌	
9	鐘	金	
		童	立
			里
10	过	寸	
		辶	

11	分	
12	刻	亥（ 、 一 亠 亥 亥 亥 ）
		刂
13	差	、 丷 丷 丷 半 美 羊 差
14	忙	忄
		亡（ 、 亠 亡 ）
15	現	王（ 一 二 千 王 ）
		見 → 目
		→ 儿
16	时	日
		寸
17	候	亻 个 仃 仁 候

Lesson 26

生詞　Shēngcí　New Words

SIDE SIX, BAND THREE

1.	能	(能动) néng	to be able, can
2.	会	(能动) huì	can, may
3.	要	(动、能动) yào	to want, should
4.	应該	(能动) yīnggāi	should, ought
5.	用	(动) yòng	to use
6.	字典	(名) zìdiǎn	dictionary
7.	認識	(动、名) rènshí	to know, to recognize
8.	还	(副) hái	also, too, still
9.	以后	(副) yǐhòu	afterwards
10.	买	(动) mǎi	to buy
11.	听	(动) tīng	to hear, to listen to
12.	好看	(形) hǎokàn	good-looking
13.	没关系	méiguānxì	never mind, it does n't matter
14.	觉得	(动) juédé	to feel
15.	东西	(名) dōngxì	thing

語法　Yǔfǎ　Grammar

26.1　Optative Verbs (verbs of ability and willingness)
Optative verbs belong to the part of speech of verbs. But they are different from other common verbs, because they have their own grammatical characteristics: they are never used redu-

plicatively and never followed by any suffix or any substantive object; they are used before verbs or adjectives. The main function of optative verbs is to indicate possibility, ability, willingness, demand or intention.

(1) 能 能 implies subjective ability. e. g.

1. 他 一天 能 看 一本 中文 書.
   Tā yìtiān néng kàn yìběn zhōngwén shū.

   He can read a Chinese book in one day.

2. 我 十分鐘 能 寫 很 多 汉字.
   Wǒ shífēnzhōng néng xiě hěn duō hànzì.

   I can write many Chinese characters in fifteen minutes (time).

Sometimes it implies permission under certain conditions. e.g.

3. 我們 不 能 在 圖書館里 説 話.
   Wǒmen bù néng zài túshūguǎnlǐ shuō huà.

   We cannot talk in the library.

4. 我 能 跟 你 一起 作 練習 嗎?
   Wǒ néng gēn nǐ yìqǐ zuò liànxí mǎ?

   Can I (OR: May I) do the exercise (together) with you?

(2) 会 会 is a verb, but it is also an optative verb used before a verb or an adjective. When it is used as an optative verb, it also implies subjective ability, but it is different from 能, because 会 means a certain skill acquired through learning, so it is often similar to 精通 (to be well-versed) and 掌握 (to master) in meaning. e. g.

5. 他 会 説 中文.
   Tā huì shuō zhōngwén.

   He can (OR: knows how to) speak Chinese.

6. 这个 同志 会 跳 舞.
   Zhèige tóngzhì huì tiào wǔ.

   This comrade can dance.

説中文 and 跳舞 in the above examples are skills acquired through learning.

会 sometimes implies a possibility under certain conditions. e. g.

7. 这本　杂誌　不　会　是　他的.
Zhèiběn　zázhì　bú　huì　shì　tādě.
This magazine can't be his.

8. 他　在　礼堂　看　电影,　不　会　在
Tā　zài　lǐtáng　kàn　diànyǐng,　bú　huì　zài
圖書館.
túshūguǎn.
He is seeing a film in the auditorium, he can't be in the library.

(3) 要　Like the word 会, 要 is a verb. e. g.

9. 先生　要　一張　干淨　紙.
Xiānshěng　yào　yìzhāng　gānjìng　zhǐ.
The teacher wants a clean sheet of paper.

When 要 is used as an optative verb, it indicates subjective desire or intention. e. g.

10. 我　要　去　圖書館.
Wǒ　yào　qù　túshūguǎn.
I want to go to the library.

11. 先生　要　看　你的　本子.
Xiānshěng　yào　kàn　nǐdě　běnzi.
The teacher wants to look at your notebook.

It sometimes indicates objective necessity.

12. 学生　要　好好兒地　学習.
Xuéshěng　yào　hǎohāordě　xuéxí.
A student must study very well.

13. 黑板　要　干淨.
Hēibǎn　yào　gānjìng.

The blackboard must be clean.

Note: 要 in example 13 is used before an adjective.

(4) 应該　应該 expresses some demand or necessity dictated by reason or habit. That is to say, it is not right or proper not to do so. e. g.

14. 我們　应該　看　这本　杂誌.
Wǒmen　yīnggāi　kàn　zhèiběn　zázhì.

We ought to read this magazine.

15. 学生　都　应該　努力.
Xuéshēng　dōu　yīnggāi　nǔlì.

All students ought to be diligent.

Note: The optative verb 应該 may be followed by an adjective.

26.2 Some Rules Concerning Optative Verbs

(1) If an optative verb is used in the alternative interrogative sentence, we need only give both the affirmative and the negative forms of the optative verb. e. g.

16. 你　能　不　能　来?
Nǐ　néng　bù　néng　lái?

Can you come (or not)?

17. 你　要　不　要　跟　我　一起　去?
Nǐ　yào　bú　yào　gēn　wǒ　yìqǐ　qù?

Do you want to go (together) with me?

If the predicate is simple and short, the element after the optative verb may be used two times. e. g.

18. 你　能　来　不　能　(来)?
Nǐ　néng　lái　bù　néng　(lái)?

Can you come?

Note: In such interrogative sentences, the optative verb has to be repeated. So we cannot say 能来不来. But the second form of the verb may be omitted.

(2) In answering questions, the optative verb may stand alone and be used as the predicate. e. g.

19. 你　要　看　报　吗?
Nǐ　yào　kàn　bào　mǎ?

Do you want to read the newspaper?

20. 要.
Yào.

Yes (I want to).

21. 你　会　不　会　用　中文　字典?
Nǐ　huì　bú　huì　yòng　zhōngwén　zìdiǎn?

Do you know how to use a Chinese dictionary?

22. 会.
Huì.

Yes.

(3) Two optative verbs may be used in succession. e. g.

23. 学生　应该　会　念　这些　汉字.
Xuéshēng　yīnggāi　huì　niàn　zhèixiē　hànzì.

Students ought to be able to read these characters.

24. 他　今天　沒　有　工作,　应该　能
Tā　jīntiān　méi　yǒu　gōngzuò,　yīnggāi　néng

来.
lái.

He has no work to do today, he should be able to come.

課文 Kèwén Text

SIDE SIX, BAND THREE

(a₁) 現在 你們 能 看 中文 报 嗎?
Xiànzài nǐmén néng kàn zhōngwén bào må?

Can you read a Chinese newspaper now?

(b₁) 不 能, 我們 只 認識 很 少的
Bù néng, wǒmén zhǐ rènshì hěn shǎodě

汉字, 还 不 能 看 报.
hànzì, hái bù néng kàn bào.

No, we recognize only a few characters, and we still can't read a newspaper.

(a₂) 你們 会 用 字典 不 会?
Nǐmén huì yòng zìdiǎn bú huì?

Do you know how to use a dictionary?

(b₂) 現在 还 不 会, 以后 先生 要
Xiànzài hái bú huì, yǐhòu xiānshěng yào

教 我們. 我們 应該 会 用 字典.
jiāo wǒmén. Wǒmén yīnggāi huì yòng zìdiǎn.

We still don't know (how); later the teacher intends to teach us (how). We ought to know how to use a dictionary.

(a₃) 你 有 沒 有 字典?
Nǐ yǒu méi yǒu zìdiǎn?

Do you have a dictionary?

(b₃) 沒 有, 我 一定 要 买 一本.
Méi yǒu, wǒ yídìng yào mǎi yìběn.

我 学習 中文, 应該 有 字典.
Wǒ xuéxí zhōngwén, yīnggāi yǒu zìdiǎn.

No, (but) I surely intend to buy one. I study Chinese, and I ought to have a dictionary.

(a₄) 你們　学習　中文，只　要　会　说
　　　 Nǐmen　xuéxí　zhōngwén, zhǐ　yào　huì　shuō

話、会　看　書　嗎?
huà、huì　kàn　shū　ma?

You are studying Chinese; do you want to be able to speak and read only?

(b₄) 不，我們　应該　能　听、能　说、能
　　　 Bù, wǒmen　yīnggāi néng　tīng、néng shuō、néng

念、能　写.
niàn、néng　xiě.

No, we ought to be able to understand (Chinese when spoken), to speak it, to read it.and to write it.

(a₅) 你們　也　会　写　汉字　嗎?
　　　 Nǐmen　yě　huì　xiě　hànzì　ma?

Do you know how to write Chinese characters also?

(b₅) 对　了，我們　会　写　一些. 我們
　　　 Duì　le,　wǒmen　huì　xiě　yìxiē.　Wǒmen

写得　慢，写得　不　好看.
xiědé　màn,　xiědé　bù　hǎokàn.

Right, we know how to write a few. We write slowly, and don't write them well (LIT.: write not good-looking).

(a₆) 沒　关系，你們　常常　練習，一定
　　　 Méi　guānxì,　nǐmen chángcháng liànxí,　yídìng

能　写得　很　好. 你們　觉得
néng　xiědé　hěn　hǎo.　Nǐmen　juédé

怎么样? 很　忙　嗎?
zěnmóyàng? Hěn　máng　ma?

No matter, practice often and you will certainly be able to write them well. How do you feel? Very busy?

(b₆)　我們　　很　　忙.　　我們　　一年　　要
　　　Wǒmén　hěn　máng.　Wǒmén　yìnián　yào

　　　学習　　很　　多　　东西,　　我們　　应該
　　　xuéxí　hěn　duō　dōngxi,　wǒmén　yīnggāi

　　　忙.
　　　máng.

We are very busy. We want to learn many things in one year, and we should be busy.

課外練習　Kèwài liànxí　Home Work

1) Write questions with each of the following words, and after that answer them:

　　(1) 能　　　　　(2) 会

　　(3) 要　　　　　(4) 应該

2) Transcribe the following Chinese characters, and compare the different pronunciation of each group:

　　(5) 以　　意

　　(6) 看　　干

　　(7) 知　　只　　枝　　誌　　紙　　志

汉字表　Hànzì biǎo　Chinese Characters

l	能	ㄙ	
		月	
		ヒ（レ ヒ）	
		ヒ	

2	要	西					
		女					
3	应	广 广 庀 应 应					
4	該	言					
		亥					
5	用	) 刀 刀 月 用					
6	典	、 冂 曰 曲 曲 典 典					
7	認	言					
		忍	刃 (刀 刃)				
			心				
8	識	言					
		戠	音	立			
				日			
		戈					
9	还	不					
		辶					
10	以	レ レ い 以					
11	买	乛 宀 乊 亞 亞 买					
12	听	口					
		斤					
13	关						

14	系	ノ ㄠ 幺 糸 系
15	觉	⿰
		见
16	东	一 ㄓ 左 𠂇 东
17	西	

Lesson 27

生詞　Shēngcí　New Words

SIDE SIX, BAND FOUR

1.	上(星期)	(形)	shàng (xīngqī)	last (week)
2.	下(星期)	(形)	xià (xīngqī)	next (week)
3.	了	(尾、助)	lē	(a suffix and a particle)
4.	从前	(副)	cóngqián	in the past, formerly
5.	明天	(名)	míngtiån	tomorrow
6.	昨天	(名)	zuótiån	yesterday
7.	回	(动)	huí	to go back, to return
8.	句子	(名)	jùzĭ	sentence
9.	就	(副)	jiù	then, at once,
10.	呢	(助)	nē	(a particle)
11.	講	(动)	jiǎng	to explain, to give a lecture on, to tell
12.	清楚	(形)	qīngchŭ	clear
13.	复习	(动)	fùxí	to review
14.	词彙	(名)	cíhuì	vocabulary
15.	語法	(名)	yŭfá	grammar
16.	进	(动)	jìn	to enter
17.	城	(名)	chéng	city, town

語法: Yǔfǎ Grammar

27.1 **The Perfective Aspect** In Chinese, the time of an action, whether it is of the past, present or future, is expressed mainly by a word or word group of time. e. g.

1. 我們　上星期六　看　电影，　你們
   Wǒmén shàngxīngqīliù kàn diànyǐng, nǐmén

下星期六　看　电影.
xiàxīngqīliù kàn diànyǐng.

We saw a film last Saturday, you (plural) will see a film next Saturday.

The time of action is indicated by the adverbial modifiers of time 上星期六 and 下星期六. The verb 看 has nothing in its morphology to express the time.

But in Chinese, the aspect of an action is very important. An action may be in its starting, progressive, continuous or completed state, and a verb may have various kinds of aspects accordingly. In today's lesson, we will discuss only the perfective aspect. In Chinese, aspects are shown by suffixes and the suffix 了 is used to indicate the aspect of a completed action. When we wish to stress the completion of an action, we use the suffix 了 after the verb. e. g.

2. 他　来　了.
   Tā lái lê.

He has come. (OR: He came.)

3. 我們　懂　了.
   Wǒmén dǒng lê.

We understand (= We have understood).

There are two points to be noticed with regard to the perfective aspect:

(1) The suffix 了 does not indicate past time. Even if the time of an action is in the past, we do not use the suffix 了, unless we want to emphasize the completion of the action. e. g.

4. 他　一九五四年　在　这兒　工作.
Tā　yījiǔwǔsìnián　zài　zhèr　gōngzuò.
He worked here in 1954.

5. 从前　他　常常　来.
Cóngqián　tā　chángcháng　lái.
In the past he came frequently. (or: He used to come
often before.)

(2) The suffix 了 may also be used to stress the completion
of an action in the future. e. g.

6. 明天　你們　来了, 我們　一起　跳　舞.
Míngtiǎn　nímèn　láilě,　wǒměn　yìqǐ　tiào wǔ.
When you (plural) come tomorrow, we will dance
together. (LIT.: Tomorrow you come-COMPLETION, we
together dance.)

This kind of perfective aspect is generally used to show the
order of actions in a sentence, for the second action only happens after the completion of the first one.

27.2 了 and the Object   When we use the suffix 了 in a
sentence in which there is an object, the following three points
have to be observed:

(1) 了 is generally used after the verb and before the
object, especially when the object is modified by an adjective
modifier. e. g.

7. 我　昨天　买了　一本　画报.
Wǒ　zuótiǎn　mǎilě　yìběn　huàbào.
Yesterday I bought a picture news magazine.

8. 星期日　我　看了　那本　杂誌.
Xīngqīrì　wǒ　kànlě　nèiběn　zázhì.
I read that magazine on Sunday.

(2) In a simple sentence, the suffix 了 is used after the
verb, and the modal particle 了 is used after the object. e. g.

9. 昨天　我　作(了)　練習　了.
Zuótiǎn　wǒ　zuò(lě)　liànxí　lě.

I did the exercises yesterday.

10. 他　回(了)　宿舍　了.
Tā　huí(lě)　sùshè　lě.

He has returned to the dormitory.

In such sentences, the suffix 了 may be omitted, the particle 了 then takes on the meaning of completion. But notice the use of 了, when the object is preceded by a numeral and a measure word. When there is only the suffix 了, we mean that the action is already concluded; when both the suffix 了 and the particle 了 are used at the same time, we mean that the action is still in progression or is being continued. e. g.

11. 我　昨天　作了　八个　句子.
Wǒ　zuótiǎn　zuòlě　bágě　jùzi.

I did eight sentences yesterday.

12. 我　作了　八个　句子　了, 现在
Wǒ　zuòlě　bágě　jùzi　lě, xiànzài

要　作　下边兒的.
yào　zuò　xiàbiǎnrdě.

I have done eight sentences (so far), now I want to do the following ones.

(3) If there is only the suffix 了 after the verb and no particle 了 after a simple object, the sentence is not complete and must be completed by adding other elements. e. g.

13. 我　作了　練習　就　去.
Wǒ　zuòlě　liànxí　jiù　qù.

After I finish the exercises I will go. (LIT.: I do-COM-PLETION exercises then go.)

14. 他　学了　中文　就　能　看　中文
Tā　xuéle　zhōngwén　jiù　néng　kàn　zhōngwén
書.
shū.

After he learns Chinese he will be able to read Chinese books.

Here the adverb 就 is always used to express successive actions or the relation of cause and effect.

27.3 **The Negative Form of the Perfective Aspect**   When we wish to express an action that did not take place, we have only to add 沒有 before the verb. e. g.

15. 昨天　他　沒（有）来.
Zuótiān　tā　méi　yǒu　lái.

He didn't come yesterday.

16. 星期六　我　沒（有）去　圖書館.
Xīngqīliù　wǒ　méi　(yǒu)　qù　túshūguǎn.

I didn't go to the library on Saturday.

We have to pay attention to the fact that the affirmative suffix 了 can never be used simultaneously with 沒有, which is the negative form of the perfective aspect.   Therefore, we must not say: 昨天他沒(有)来了 or 星期六我沒(有)去了圖書館.

If an action is not yet completed, and is to be completed very soon, we use the construction 还沒(有)...呢 (not yet...), the 呢 here is a modal particle. e. g.

17. 我　今天　还　沒（有）看　报　呢!
Wǒ　jīntiān　hái　méi　(yǒu)　kàn　bào　ne!

I have not yet read the newspaper today.

沒有 may be always shortened as 沒, whenever it is used before a verb, but when 沒有 is used independently to answer a question, it should never be shortened. e. g.

18. 先生　来　了　嗎?
Xiānshēng　lái　le　ma?

Has the teacher come?

19. 沒 有.

     Méi   yǒu.

     No (He hasn't).

20. 沒 来.

     Méi   lái.

     No (He hasn't come).

21. 还 沒 (有) 来 呢!

     Hái méi (yǒu) lái nêl

     Not yet (He hasn't come yet).

27.4 The Alternative Interrogative Sentence of the Perfective Aspect If we wish to ask a question using the alternative interrogative sentence, we have only to use this sentence pattern ......了 (object) 沒有. e. g.

22. 报 来 了 沒 有?

     Bào lái lê méi yǒu?

     Has the newspaper come (or not)?

23. 你 作了 練習 沒 有?

     Nǐ zuòlê liànxí méi yǒu?

     Have you done the exercises?

Here 沒有 cannot be shortened as 沒 either.

課文 Kèwén Text

SIDE SIX, BAND FOUR

I

(a₁) 今天的 練習 有 八个 句子, 你

     Jīntiāndê liànxí yǒu bágê jùzǐ, nǐ

作了 几个 了?

zuòlê jǐgê lê?

There are eight sentences in today's exercise; how many have you done?

(b₁) 作了　四个　了.
　　　Zuòle　sìgê　le.

I've done four.

(a₂) 你　会　作　后边兒的　那　四个　吗?
　　　Nǐ　huì　zuò　hòubiānrde　nèi　sìge　ma?

Do you know how to do those four that come later?

(b₂) 先生　講得　很　清楚,　我　都　懂
　　　Xiānsheng jiǎngde　hěn　qīngchǔ,　wǒ　dōu　dǒng

了,　我　会　作.
le,　wǒ　huì　zuò.

The teacher explained them very clearly and I understood everything, so I know how to do them.

(a₃) 你　复習了　从前的　詞彙　沒　有?
　　　Nǐ　fùxíle　cóngqiánde　cíhuì　méi　yǒu?

Have you reviewed the previous vocabulary words?

(b₃) 还　沒　有　复習　呢!　我　明天　复習.
　　　Hái　méi　yǒu　fùxí　ne!　Wǒ　míngtiān　fùxí.

Not yet. I'll review them tomorrow.

(a₄) 复習了　詞彙,　你　作　什么?
　　　Fùxíle　cíhuì,　nǐ　zuò　shénmo?

After you review the vocabulary, what will you do?

(b₄) 复習了　詞彙,　我　就　复習　語法.
　　　Fùxíle　cíhuì,　wǒ　jiù　fùxí　yǔfǎ.

After I review the vocabulary, I will then review the grammar.

(a₅) 复習了　詞彙　和　語法,　你　还　要　作
　　　Fùxíle　cíhuì　hé　yǔfǎ,　nǐ　hái　yào　zuò

什么?
shénmo?

After you review the vocabulary and the grammar, what else do you intend to do?

(b₅) 复習了　詞彙　和　語法，我　就　練習
Fùxíle　cíhuì　hé　yǔfǎ，wǒ　jiù　liànxí

汉字．
hànzì.

After I review the vocabulary and the grammar, I will then practice the characters.

II

(a₆) 上星期六　你　作　什么　了？
Shàngxīngqīliù　nǐ　zuò　shénmǒ　le?

What did you do last Saturday?

(b₆) 我　进　城　了．
Wǒ　jìn　chéng　le.

I went into the city.

(a₇) 你　在　城里　看了　电影　没　有？
Nǐ　zài　chénglǐ　kànle　diànyíng　méi　yǒu?

Did you see a film in the city?

(b₇) 没　有，我　买　东西　了．
Méi　yǒu，wǒ　mǎi　dōngxī　le.

No, I went shopping (LIT.: bought things).

(a₈) 你　买　什么　东西　了？
Nǐ　mǎi　shénmǒ　dōngxī　le?

What (things) did you buy?

(b₈) 我　买了　一本　字典　和　很　多　杂誌．
Wǒ　mǎile　yìběn　zìdiǎn　hé　hěn　duō　zázhì.

I bought a dictionary and a lot of magazines.

(a₉) 你　没（有）买　書　嗎？
Nǐ　méi　(yǒu)　mǎi　shū　ma?

Didn't you buy books?

(b₉) 沒　有.

Méi　yǒu.

No.

課外練習　Kèwài liànxí　Home Work

1) Re-write the following sentences using Chinese characters and underline the suffix 了:

(1) Zhèigê yuêdê "Rénmín Huàbào" lái lê.

(2) Wǒ zuòlê liànxí jiù gēn nî chàng gēr.

(3) Tā xīngqīrì méi yǒu jìn chéng, zài xuéxiào fùxí yǔfǎ lê.

2) Answer the following questions in the negative:

(4) 你　同屋　回　宿舍　了　沒　有?

(5) 先生　講　这些　句子　了　嗎?

(6) 他　用了　这本　字典　沒　有?

3) Complete the following sentences:

(7) 听了　唱　歌兒...

(8) 我　进了　圖書館...

汉字表　Hànzì biǎo　Chinese Characters

1	明	日			
		月			
2	昨	日			
		乍			
3	回	丨	冂	冋	回
4	句	丿	勺	句	
5	就	京			
		尤（一 ナ 尢 尤）			

6	呢		
7	講	言	
		冓 (一 二 丰 井 坓 菁 菁 冓)	
8	清	氵	
		青	
9	楚	林	木
			木
		疋 (一 丁 下 疋 疋)	
10	复	ノ 一 百 旬 复	
11	詞	言	
		司 (门 刁 司)	
12	彙	ク タ 夕 备 彙	
13	語	言	
		吾	五
			口
14	法	氵	
		去	
15	进		
16	城	土	
		成 (厂 万 成 成 成)	

Lesson 28

生詞　Shēngcí　New Words

SIDE SIX, BAND FIVE

1.	开始	(动)	kāishǐ	to start, to begin
2.	住	(动)	zhù	to live, to dwell
3.	上(課)	(动)	shàng(kè)	to go to class, to attend class
4.	字	(名)	zì	character
5.	...的时候兒		...dèshíhôur	when..., at the time of
6.	下(課)	(动)	xià(kè)	the class is over, after class
7.	从...起		cóng...qǐ	since..., from the time of
8.	上(月)	(形)	shàng(yuè)	last month, ultimo
9.	从...到...		cóng...dào...	from...to...
10.	已經	(副)	yǐjīng	already
11.	节	(量)	jié	(a measure word)
12.	課	(名)	kè	lesson, class
13.	翻譯	(动、名)	fānyì	to translate, to interpret translation, interpretation, interpreter
14.	特別	(形)	tèbié	special, particular
15.	帮助	(动)	bāngzhù	to help
16.	教室	(名)	jiàoshǐ	classroom
17.	休息	(动)	xiūxi	rest, to take a rest

語法 Yǔfǎ Grammar

28.1 The Structural Particle 的 (2) We have already learned that when a noun, pronoun or adjective is used to make up an adjective modifier, it is necessary to use the structural particle 的 to join the adjective modifier and the central word together (15.1). Here we shall discuss those adjective modifiers that are made up of verbs, verbal constructions, or subject-predicate constructions (clauses). First of all, let us see how a verb becomes an adjective modifier. e. g.

1. 这本 字典 很 好, 买 的 人 很 多.
   Zhèiběn zìdiǎn hěn hǎo, mǎi dě rén hěn duō.

   This dictionary is very good, and many people buy it (LIT.: buy PARTICLE people very many).

The word 买 in the above example is a simple verb used as adjective modifier. Now let us see how verbal constructions become adjective modifiers. e. g.

2. 上星期 来 的 学生 开始 学习 了.
   Shàngxīngqī lái dě xuéshēng kāishǐ xuéxí lě.

   The student who came last week (LIT.: last week come PARTICLE student) has begun to study.

3. 他 是 从 城里 来 的 那个 同志.
   Tā shì cóng chénglǐ lái dě nèigě tóngzhì.

   He is that comrade who came from the city. (LIT.: He is from city-in come PARTICLE that comrade.)

4. 来得 早 的 人 都 在 前边兒.
   Láidě zǎo dě rén dōu zài qiánbiānr.

   All the people who came early are in the front.

5. 她 是 教 语法 的 先生.
   Tā shì jiāo yǔfǎ dě xiānshēng.

   She is the teacher who teaches grammar.

Here, 上星期来 is an adj. modifier composed of a verb and its adverbial modifier, 从城里来 is an adjective modifier composed of a verb and a prepositional construction (phrase) modifying the verb, 来得早 is an adj. modifier composed of a verb and its complement, and 教語法 is an adj. modifier composed of a verb and its object. Although all the above adj. modifiers are composed of different constructions, yet, the one common feature is that in each of them the verb is used as the main element. Therefore, they are all verbal constructions used as adj. modifiers.

Last of all, let us see how subject-predicate constructions become adj. modifiers. Such modifiers may be divided into two kinds:

(1) The construction in which the predicate is composed mainly of an adjective. e. g.

6. 中文 不 好 的 人 不 会 用 这本
   Zhōngwén bù hǎo dě rén bú huì yòng zhèiběn

字典.
zìdiǎn.

Those who are not good in Chinese (LIT.: Chinese-language not good PARTICLE people) do not know how to use this dictionary.

7. 他 是 一个 工作 积极的 同志.
   Tā shì yígě gōngzuò jījídě tóngzhì.

He is a comrade who works enthusiastically.

中文不好 and 工作积极 are subject-predicate constructions used as adjective modifiers and the adjectives 好 and 积极 are predicates.

(2) The construction in which the predicate is composed mainly of a verb. e. g.

8. 我 喜欢 他 买 的 那本 書.
   Wǒ xǐhuǎn tā mǎi dě nèiběn shū.

I like that book he bought. (LIT.: I like he bought PARTICLE that book.)

9. 他們   復習   <u>先生   講</u>   的   語法.
Tāmén   fùxí   xiānshěng jiǎng   dě   yǔfǎ.

They reviewed the grammar which the teacher explained (lectured).

他买 and 先生講 are all subject-predicate constructions used as adjective modifiers, and the verbs 买 and 講 are predicates. Notice: such constructions cannot be used independently as complete sentences.

Besides, there is another kind of subject-predicate construction that is complete in meaning by itself, where the verb may or may not carry an object. It is a complete sentence by itself. e. g.

10. <u>他   學習</u>   的   那本   中文   書   是
Tā   xuéxí   dě   nèiběn   zhōngwén   shū   shì

他們的   先生   寫的.
tāměndě   xiānshěng   xiědě.

That Chinese book he is studying was written by their teacher. (LIT.: He studies PARTICLE that Chinese book is their teacher wrote one.)

11. 哪兒   是   <u>他們   上   課</u>   的   地方?
Nǎr   shì   tāměn   shàng   kè   dě   dìfāng?

Where do they attend class? (LIT.: Where is they attend class PARTICLE place?)

In all the above sentences, the structural particle 的 has to be inserted between the adjective modifiers and the central words.

When the central words are clearly understood from the context, all the above central words modified by adjective modifiers can be omitted. e. g.

12. 他們   都   在   那兒: <u>說   話</u>   的   是
Tāměn   dōu   zài   nàr: shuō   huà   dě   shì

先生,   <u>寫   字</u>   的   是   學生.
xiānshěng,   xiě   zì   dě   shì   xuéshěng.

They are all there: the one talking is the teacher, the ones writing characters are the students.

13. 我 給 他 的 是 一本 書.
Wǒ gěi tā dě shì yìběn shū.

It was a book that I gave him. (LIT.: I gave him PAR-
TICLE is one book.)

In example 12, 人 has been omitted and in example 13 东西
has been omitted.

28.2 ...的时候兒   This is a very common construction
eqivalent to the English "when" or "at the time of...". In
general, it is placed after a word or a complicated construction
used as adverbial modifier. e. g.

14. 工作 的 时候兒, 他 一定 好好兒地
Gōngzuò dě shíhòur, tā yídìng hǎohāordě

工作.
gōngzuò.

When he works, he certainly works very well.

15. 作 練習 的 时候兒, 他 写 汉字
Zuò liànxí dě shíhòur, tā xiě hànzì

写得 很 清楚.
xiědě hěn qīngchǔ.

When he does his exercises, he writes the characters
very clearly.

16. 我 回 宿舍 的 时候兒, 他 还
Wǒ huí sùshè dě shíhòur, tā hái

沒 下 課 呢!
méi xià kè ně!

When I returned to the dormitory, he was not yet
finished with his class.

28.3 从...起   It is also a common construction used as
adverbial modifier of time. e. g.

17. 他們 从 上月 起 学習 中文.
Tāměn cóng shàngyuè qǐ xuéxí zhōngwén.

They have been studying Chinese since last month.

18. 我們 从 学習 語法 起, 作了 很
　　Wǒmen cóng xuéxí yǔfǎ qǐ, zuòle hěn

　　多 練習 了.
　　duō liànxí le.

Since we studied the grammar, we have been doing many exercises.

19. 从 我 認識 他 起, 我們 常常
　　Cóng wǒ rènshi tā qǐ, wǒmen chángcháng

　　一起 学習.
　　yìqǐ xuéxí.

Since I met him, we have often studied together.

From the above examples, we see that we may either insert a word or a complicated construction into this construction.

28.4 从...到... This is also a common construction used as adverbial modifier of time. e. g.

20. 我們 从 七点半 到 十点半 学習.
　　Wǒmen cóng qīdiǎnbàn dào shídiǎnbàn xuéxí.
　　We studied from 7:30 to 10:30.

21. 他 从 一九五二年 到 一九五五年
　　Tā cóng yījiǔwǔèrnián dào yījiǔwǔwǔnián

　　在 北京 大学 工作.
　　zài Běijīng Dàxué gōngzuò.

He worked at Peking University from 1952 to 1955.

But, it may also be used as adjective modifier indicating limit or scope. e. g.

22. 星期六 我們 复習 从 星期一 到
　　Xīngqīliù wǒmen fùxí cóng xīngqīyī dào

　　星期五 的 語法.
　　xīngqīwǔ de yǔfǎ.

On Saturday we reviewed the grammar from Monday's to Friday's (grammar).

課文　Kèwén　Text
SIDE SIX, BAND FIVE

I

上星期　我　看了　你　給　我　的
Shàngxīngqī　wǒ　kànlê　nǐ　gěi　wǒ　dê

那本　画报.　你　給　我　的　那本　画报
nèibēn　huàbào.　Nǐ　gěi　wǒ　dê　nèibēn　huàbào

很　有意思,　不　会　中文　的　人　也
hěn　yǒuyìsî,　bú　huì　zhōngwén　dê　rén　yě

能　看　那本　画报.
néng　kàn　nèibēn　huàbào.

Last week I read that picture news magazine you gave
me. That picture news magazine you gave me is very
interesting; even people who don't know Chinese can
read that picture news magazine.

II

他們　从　上星期　起,　已經　开始　学
Tāmên　cóng　shàngxīngqī　qǐ,　yǐjīng　kāishî　xué-

習　了.　从　八点　(过)　五分　到　十一点
xi　lê.　Cóng　bādiǎn　(guò)　wǔfēn　dào　shíyīdiǎn

四十分,　他們　有　四节　課.　上　課　的
sìshîfēn,　tāmên　yǒu　sìjié　kè.　Shàng　kè　dê

时候兒,　先生　説　中文　説得　很　慢、很
shíhôur,　xiānshêng　shuō　zhōngwén　shuōdê　hěn　màn、hěn

清楚,　他們　都　能　懂　先生　説　的　話.
qīngchû,　tāmên　dōu　néng　dông　xiānshêng　shuō　dê　huà.

复習　的　时候兒,　作　翻譯　工作　的　同志
Fùxi　dê　shíhôur,　zuò　fānyî　gōngzuò　dê　tóngzhì

还　特別　帮助　他們.
hái　tèbié　bāngzhû　tāmên.

Since last week they have already begun to study.
From five after eight to eleven-forty they have four
classes. During the classes, the teacher speaks Chinese
very slowly and clearly, and they all are able to under-

stand everything the teacher says. When they review,
the comrade who does translation (work) gives them
special help also.

III

从	苏联	来	的	学生	都	在	这个
Cóng	Sūlián	lái	dě	xuéshěng	dōu	zài	zhèigè

宿舍里	住.	他們	上	課	的	教室	在
sùshèlǐ	zhù.	Tāmén	shàng	kè	dě	jiàoshǐ	zài

宿舍	旁边兒.	下	課	的	时候兒,	他們
sùshè	pángbiānr.	Xià	kè	dě	shíhòur,	tāmén

都	在	教室	外边兒	休息.	休息	的
dōu	zài	jiàoshǐ	wàibiānr	xiūxi.	Xiūxi	dě

时候兒,	先生	看	画报,	学生	唱	歌兒.
shíhòur,	xiānshēng	kàn	huàbào,	xuéshěng	chàng	gēr.

先生	都	喜欢	看	"人民	画报",	学生
Xiānshēng	dōu	xǐhuǎn	kàn	"Rénmín	Huàbào",	xuéshěng

都	喜欢	唱	張	同志	教	他們	的
dōu	xǐhuǎn	chàng	Zhāng	tóngzhì	jiāo	tāmén	dě

中文	歌兒.
zhōngwén	gēr.

All the students from the Soviet Union live in this
dormitory. The classroom where they meet is next to
the dormitory. When the class is over, they all rest
outside the classroom. During the rest period, the
teacher reads picture news magazines and the students sing. The teachers like to read "The People's
Picture Magazine" and the students like to sing Chinese songs which Comrade Chāng taught them.

課外練習　Kèwài liànxí　Home Work

1) Translate the following sentences into Chinese:

(1) Those who want to see the film have already gone
to the city.

(2) The newspaper he is now reading (literally to see) is
yesterday's.

(3) Students who are good in English may read the English magazines.

(4) The place where we are resting is beside the auditorium.

2) Copy the following sentences and fill the blanks with either 得 or 的:

(5) 学习＿＿多 的 学生 应该 帮助
学习得 少＿＿学生.

(6) 我 同屋 买＿＿东西 都 在 桌子上.

(7) 我 写 从前 学＿＿词彙, 写＿＿快;
我 写 今天 学＿＿词彙, 写＿＿.慢

汉字表　Hànzì biǎo　Chinese Characters

1	开	二 于 开	
2	始	女	
		台	厶
			口
3	住	亻	
		主 (丶 二 三 于 主)	
4	課	言	
		果 (曰 旦 果)	
5	到	至	
		刂	
6	己	㇕ 𠃍 己	

7	經	糸		
		巠 (一 ㄍ ㄍㄍ ㄍ 巠)		
8	节	艹		
		卩 (ㄱ 卩)		
9	翻	番	釆 (ノ ㄑ ㄓ 乎 乎 釆)	
			田	
		羽		
10	譯	言		
		睪	四	
			幸 (土 士 圥 圥 幸)	
11	特	牛 (ノ 二 牛 牛)		
		寺	土	
			寸	
12	別	另	口	
			力	
		刂		
13	幫	邦 (一 二 三 丰 邦)		
		巾		
14	助	且 (ㅣ 冂 月 月 且)		
		力		

15	室	宀
		至
16	休	亻
		木
17	息	自（丿自）
		心

Lesson 29

生詞 Shēngcí New Words

1. 还是　　（連）háishì　　　　　or
2. 每　　　（代）měi　　　　　　each, every
3. 生詞　　（名）shēngcí　　　　new word
4. 小説兒　（名）xiǎoshuōr [本] novel
5. 借　　　（动）jiè　　　　　　to lend, to borrow
6. 想　　　（动、能动）xiǎng　 to think, to want, to intend
7. 还　　　（动）huán　　　　　to return, to give back
8. 可以　　（能动）kěyǐ　　　　may
9. 謝謝　　　　　 xièxiě　　　　to thank, thanks
10. 問　　　（动）wèn　　　　　to ask, to inquire
11. 問題　　（名）wèntí　　　　question, problem
12. 必須　　（能动）bìxū　　　　must, have to
13. 回答　　（动、名）huídá　　 to answer, to reply
14. 对　　　（形）duì　　　　　right, correct
15. 告訴　　（动）gàosù　　　　to tell, to inform
16. 方法　　（名）fāngfǎ　　　　way, method

語法 Yǔfǎ Grammar

29.1 **The Inversion of Object**　We know already that in Chinese the general word order of the sentence with a verbal predicate is:

(Adj. modifier) Subject — (Adverbial modifier) Verb — (Adj. modifier) Object

But the object can be put before the subject under certain conditions. Here we shall introduce two kinds of sentences with inverted object:

(1) In a sentence in which the predicate is comparatively complicated (or when the object consists of several words), the sentence becomes more compact and clearer in meaning, if the object is transposed to the beginning of the sentence. e. g.

1. 中文 書 我 朋友 看得 很 快.
   Zhōngwén shū wǒ péngyǒu kàndé hěn kuài.

   My friend reads Chinese books very quickly. ("Chinese books" comes first)

2. 先生 説 的 話 我 听得 很 清
   Xiānshēng shuō dé huà wǒ tīngdé hěn qīng-
   楚.
   chǔ.

   I (generally) hear very clearly what the teacher says.
   (LIT.: Teacher says PARTICLE speech I hear PARTICLE very clearly.)

In each of the above two sentences, there is a complement of degree. If the objects are not transposed, the verbs have to be reduplicated. (e. g. 我朋友看中文書, 看得很快 and 我听先生的話, 听得很清楚). For the sake of compactness, the object is always put at the beginning of a sentence.

When the object is a compound object or in the plural form, the adverb 都 has to be used before the predicate. e. g.

3. 練習里的 汉字 他 都 写得 很
   Liànxílîdé hànzì tā dōu xiědé hěn
   好看.
   hǎokàn.

   He (generally) writes (all) the characters in the exercises very beautifully.

4. 我 买 的 杂誌 你 都 能 看.
Wǒ mǎi dě zázhì nǐ dōu néng kàn.
You may read (all) the magazines I bought.

(2) In order to stress the object in a sentence, we can transpose the object to the beginning of a sentence. e. g.

5. 这个 月的 人民 画报 我 已經
Zhèige yuède Rénmín Huàbào wǒ yǐjing
看 了.
kàn lě.
I have already read this month's "People's Picture Magazine."

6. 那个 新 同志的 名字 我 不 知道.
Nèige xīn tóngzhìdě míngzi wǒ bù zhīdào.
I don't know that new comrade's name.

The parallel elements in a sentence are always stressed. If they happen to be two objects, we may transpose them to the beginning of the sentence. e. g.

7. 新 杂誌 我 买, 旧 杂誌 我 不
Xīn zázhì wǒ mǎi, jiù zázhì wǒ bù
买.
mǎi.
I buy new magazines, I don't buy old magazines.

8. 昨天的 語法 他 懂, 今天的 (語法)
Zuótiānde yǔfǎ tā dǒng, jīntiānde (yǔfǎ)
他 也 懂.
tā yě dǒng.
He understands yesterday's grammar, and he understands today's (grammar) also.

The parallel elements are joined together sometimes for contrast (as in example 7) and sometimes according to the sequence of time (as in example 8). In the latter case, the adverb 也 is always used. But a compound object may be used instead of the parallel construction, if it is a kind that is based on the sequence of time. e. g.

9. 昨天的　語法　和　今天的　語法　他
Zuótiǎndě　yǔfǎ　hé　jīntiǎndě　yǔfǎ　tā

都　懂.
dōu　dǒng.

He understands (both) yesterday's grammar and to-day's grammar.

Note: When the compound object is transposed to the beginning of the sentence, the adverb 都 has to be added before the predicate.

29.2　The Interrogative Sentence (4)　The fourth kind of the interrogative sentence contains two alternative questions represented by the construction (compound conjunction) (还是)…还是…… The construction (还是)…还是 should be placed before the elements concerning which the questions are asked. e. g.

10. (还是)　你　来,　还是　她　来?
(Hái shì)　nǐ　lái,　háishì　tā　lái?

Are you coming or is she coming?

11. 你　(还是)　来,　还是　不　来?
Nǐ　(háishì)　lái,　háishì　bù　lái?

Are you coming or not (coming)?

In example 10, we wish to know "who is coming", putting 还是 before the subject of each clause; in example 11, we wish to know whether "you will come or not", with 还是 before the compound predicate.

29.3 每 includes all the individual members or elements of a group of persons or things. Two points should be noticed in using the word 每:

(1) It is a demonstrative pronoun and cannot be directly used with a noun. There should be a measure word. e. g.

12. 每个　学生　都　很　努力　学习.
Měigě　xuéshěng　dōu　hěn　nǔlì　xuéxí.

Every (OR: Each) student studies very diligently.

13. 每張　桌子　都　很　干淨.
Měizhāng zhuōzǐ dōu hěn gānjǐng.

Every table is very clean.

However, some nouns have the function of measure words, so they can be directly used with the word 每. e. g.

14. 我們　每天　八点　过　五分　上　課.
Wǒmen měitiān bādiǎn guò wǔfēn shàng kè.

We start class every day at 8:05.

15. 每課　有　十五个　生詞.
Měikè yǒu shíwǔgè shēngcí.

There are fifteen new words in every lesson.

(2) When the word 每 is used as adjective modifier of the subject, the adverb 都 is always placed before the predicate. e. g.

16. 每个　学生　都　作了　練習　了.
Měigè xuéshēng dōu zuòlè liànxí lè.

Every student has done the exercises.

17. 每(个)　人　都　应該　会　用　那
Měi(gè) rén dōu yīnggāi huì yòng nèi-
本　字典.
běn zìdiǎn.

Everybody ought to be able to use that dictionary.

But 都 may also be omitted. When such is the case 每 takes on almost the same meaning as 一. e. g.

18. 每年　有　十二个　月.
Měinián yǒu shíèrgè yuè.

There are twelve months in a (every) year.

19. 每个　学生　应該　有　两个　本子.
Měigè xuéshēng yīnggāi yǒu liǎnggè běnzi.

A (Every) student ought to have two notebooks.

課文   Kèwén   Text

SIDE SIX, BAND SIX

I

(a₁)   这   两本   小説兒   是   誰的?   是
Zhèi   liǎngběn   xiǎoshuōr   shì   shéidě?   Shì

你的,   还是   張   同志的?
nǐdě,   háishì   Zhāng   tóngzhìdě?

Who owns these two novels? Are they yours or Comrade Chāng's?

(b₁)   这本   中文的   是   張   同志的,   那本
Zhèiběn   zhōngwéndě   shì   Zhāng   tóngzhìdě,   nèiběn

俄文的   是   我   在   圖書館   借   的.
èwéndě   shì   wǒ   zài   túshūguǎn   jiè   dě.

This one in Chinese is Comrade Chāng's, that one in Russian is the one I borrowed from the library.

(a₂)   两本   你   都   看   了   嗎?
Liǎngběn   nǐ   dōu   kàn   lě   mǎ?

Have you read them both?

(b₂)   对   了,   两本   都   看   了.
Duì   lě,   liǎngběn   dōu   kàn   lě.

Right, I have read them both.

(a₃)   哪本   好?   还是   中文的   有意思,
Něiběn   hǎo?   Háishì   zhōngwéndě   yǒuyìsī,

还是   俄文的   有意思?
háishì   èwéndě   yǒuyìsī?

Which one is good? Is the Chinese one or the Russian one interesting?

(b₃) 都　有意思.　我　都　喜欢.
Dōu　yǒuyìsi.　Wǒ　dōu　xǐhuān.

你　想　不　想　看?
Ní　xiǎng　bù　xiǎng　kàn?

They're both interesting. I like them both. Do you want to read them?

(a₄) 俄文的　想　看,　中文的　我　还
Èwéndě　xiǎng　kàn,　zhōngwéndě　wǒ　hái

不　懂　呢!　你　哪天　还　这本
bù　dǒng　ně!　Ní　něitiān　huán　zhèiběn

俄文的?
èwéndě?

I want to read the Russian one; I wouldn't understand the Chinese one yet. On what day are you returning this Russian one?

(b₄) 下星期　还.　你　可以　在　这个
Xiàxīngqī　huán.　Ní　kěyǐ　zài　zhèigě

星期里　看.
xīngqīlǐ　kàn.

Next week. You may read it this week.

(a₅) 谢谢,　我　看了　就　还　你.
Xièxiě,　wǒ　kànlě　jiù　huán　nǐ.

Thank you, I'll read it and then return it to you.

II

(a₆) 你們　每天　上　几节　課?
Nǐmen　měitiān　shàng　jǐjié　kè?

How many classes do you have every day?

(b₆) 每天　四节.
Měitiān　sìjié.
Four a day.

(a₇) 每天　都　上　四节　课　吗?
Měitiān　dōu　shàng　sìjié　kè　må?
You have four classes a day?

(b₇) 对　了, 我們　現在　每天　都　上
Duì　lě,　wǒměn　xiànzài　měitiān　dōu　shàng
四节　课, 星期六　也　上　四节　课.
sìjié　kè,　xīngqīliù　yě　shàng　sìjié　kè.
Yes, now we have four classes a day, even on Saturday.

(a₈) 上　課　的　时候兒, 先生　問　你
Shàng　kè　dě　shíhôur,　xiānshěng　**wèn**　ni-
們　問題　吗?
měn　wèntí　må?
During the class, does the teacher ask you questions?

(b₈) 問, 他　每天　都　問.
Wèn,　tā　měitiān　dōu　wèn.
Yes, every day.

(a₉) 每个　学生　他　都　問　吗?
Měigě　xuéshěng　tā　dōu　wèn　må?
Does he question every student?

(b₉) 每个　学生　他　都　問. 每人　都
Měigě　xuéshěng　tā　dōu　wèn.　Měirén　dōu
必須　回答.
bìxū　huídá.
He questions every student. Everyone must answer.

(a₁₀) 先生的　問題　你們　都　回答得
Xiānshĕngdĕ　wèntí　nĭmĕn　dōu　huídádĕ

对　嗎?
duì　mă?

Do you answer all the teacher's questions correctly?

(b₁₀) 回答得　不　对　的　时候兒,　先
Huídádĕ　bú　duì　dĕ　shíhôur,　xiān-

生　就　告訴　我們.　这　是　練習
shĕng　jiù　gàosŭ　wŏmĕn.　Zhèi　shì　liànxí

的　好　方法.
dĕ　hăo　fāngfă.

When we don't answer correctly, then the teacher
tells us (so). This is a good method of practice.

課外練習　Kèwài liànxí　Home Work

I) Re-write the following interrogative sentences with
(还是) ⋯ 还是:

(1) 你　什么　时候兒（今天, 明天）还
他　这本　字典?

(2) 他　唱　的　是　什么（俄文的, 中文的）
歌兒?

2) Make sentences with each of the following groups of
words:

(3) 每　小說兒

(4) 每　年

(3) Change the following into sentences with inverted objects:

(5) 他　回答　先生　問　的　兩个
問題　回答得　特別　清楚.

(6) 先生　已經　告訴　我們　復習
詞彙　的　方法　了, 还　沒有　告訴
我們　复習　語法　的　方法　呢!

汉字表　Hànzì biǎo　Chinese Characters

1	每	ノ ┌ 仁 勹 每 每 每	
2	借	亻	
		昔 (一 十 卄 世 昔)	
3	想	相	木
			目
		心	
4	可		
5	謝	言	
		射	身 (ノ 亻 冂 勹 肙 身 身)
			寸
6	問		
7	題		
8	必	丶 心 心 必 必	

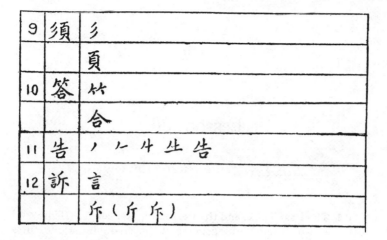

9	須	彡
		頁
10	答	竹
		合
11	告	ノ 上 牛 生 告
12	訴	言
		斤（斤 斥）

Lesson 30

語法复習　Yǔfǎ　fùxí　Review

30.1 The Past Tense and the Perfective Aspect　Time and aspect are two different things. One of the characteristic features of the Chinese language is that the morphology of a verb is not determined by time but by aspect. Let us clarify this problem by making a comparison between the past tense and the perfective aspect.

In Chinese, time is generally expressed by an adverbial modifier of time; so a past action is always shown by an adverbial modifier made up of a word or word group expressing some past time. e. g.

1. 我們　从前　常常　唱　中国　歌兒.
   Wǒmén　cóngqián　chángcháng　chàng Zhōngguó　gēr.
   In the past (Before) we often sang Chinese songs.

2. 一九五六年　他們　在　这个　工厂
   Yìjiǔwǔliùnián　tāmén　zài　zhèigè　gōngchǎng

   工作.
   gōngzuò.
   They worked in this factory in 1956.

唱中国歌兒 and 工作 are all past actions, the time of the actions being shown by the words 从前 and 1956 年. But the verbs themselves are not inflected. It is because verbs in Chinese do not change in form according to the change of time. Hence, we must never put the suffix 了 after verbs, when the actions are in the past.

In Chinese, the inflection of a verb is determined by the different state of an action. An action may be in its progressive, continuous or complete state, and the word 了 is the suffix indicating the perfective aspect. But we must pay attention to the fact that the suffix 了 is used only when we wish to lay stress on the completion of an action. When we have no wish to emphasize the completion of an action in the past, there is no need to use this suffix.

30.2 **Time of Action of the Perfective Aspect**   As mentioned above, the aspect of an action is only determined by the state of the action. Therefore, whether the action is in the past or in the future, it may have different aspects. Sentences of the perfective aspect (we have already learned these) can be classified into two kinds:

(1) When the sentence contains only one action in the past. e. g.

3. 昨天　我　<u>看了</u>　一本　小説兒.
   Zuótiān　wǒ　<u>kànlê</u>　yìběn　xiǎoshuōr.
   Yesterday I read a novel.

(2) When there are two actions in the sentence, in general, the second action takes place only after the completion of the first action. So far as time is concerned, such sentences may be subdivided into two kinds:

a) Both actions take place in the past time. e. **g.**

4. 昨天　他　<u>下了</u>　課,　很　快地　就
   Zuótiān　tā　<u>xiàlê</u>　kè,　hěn　kuàidê　jiù

   去　圖書館　<u>了.</u>
   qù　túshūguǎn　<u>lê.</u>

   Yesterday, after his class was over, he went to the library very quickly.

b) Both actions happen in the future. e. **g.**

5. 明天　我　<u>下了</u>　課,　就　回　宿舍.
   Míngtiān　wǒ　<u>xiàlê</u>　kè,　jiù　huí　sùshè.
   Tomorrow, after my class is over, I shall return to the dormitory.

We may arrive at the conclusion:

(1) In Chinese, the inflection of a verb shows aspect only; time and aspect are entirely two different things— the perfective aspect is not the same as the past tense.

(2) There is perfective aspect in the past time as well as in the future. When we wish to emphasize one future action happening after the completion of another one, the latter should be told by a verb of the perfective aspect.

30.3 不 and 沒有 These two adverbs indicate negation, but 沒有 is only used in the sentence with a verbal predicate. Here we shall deal with the negative forms of the sentence with a verbal predicate:

(1) 不 is used under the following conditions:

(a) All the customary or habitual actions, whatever the time may be, are negated by 不. e. g.

6. 從前　他　不　跳　舞.
Cóngqián　tā　bú　tiào　wú.
Formerly he didn't dance.

7. 这个　先生　不　教　我們,　那个
Zhèige　xiānshěng　bù　jiāo　wǒměn,　nèige
先生　教　我們.
xiānshěng　jiāo　wǒměn.
This teacher is not our instructor (does not teach us), that teacher is our instructor (teaches us).

(b) 不 is used to negate all future actions. e. g.

8. 星期日　我們　休息,　不　工作.
Xīngqīrì　wǒměn　xiūxí,　bù　gōngzuò.
On Sunday we rest, we do not work.

9. 下星期　他　不　进　城.
Xiàxīngqī　tā　bú　jìn　chéng.
Next week he will not go into the city.

Only when we wish to stress an action that is not yet completed, we use 沒有. e. g.

10. 我 必须 在 明天 还 没 有 上
Wǒ bìxū zài míngtiān hái méi yǒu shàng
课 的 时候 練習 这些 汉字.
kè de shíhòur liànxí zhèixiē hànzì.

Tomorrow I must practice these characters before the class begins. (LIT.: I must at tomorrow still not have attend class PARTICLE time practice these characters.)

(c) 不 is used to negate intention or wish regardless of the time. e. g.

11. 休息 的 时候兒 他 看 画报, 不
Xiūxi de shíhòur tā kàn huàbào, bú
唱歌兒.
chànggēr.

In the rest period he reads picture news magazines, he does not sing.

12. 他 不 喜欢 这个 电影, 他 不
Tā bù xǐhuān zhèigè diànyǐng, tā bú
看.
kàn.

He does not like this film, he will not see it.

(d) 不 is used before optative verbs or verbs implying mental states. e. g.

13. 开始 学习 的 时候兒, 我 不 会
Kāishǐ xuéxí de shíhòur, wǒ bú huì
說 中国 話.
shuō Zhōngguó huà.

When I began studying, I was not able to speak Chinese.

14. 他 没 有 告訴 我, 我 不 知道.
Tā méi yǒu gàosu wǒ, wǒ bù zhīdào.

He didn't tell me, I don't know.

(2) 没有 is used to show that a certain action has not happened. e. g.

15. 我　同屋　还　没　有　回　宿舍　呢!
Wǒ　tóngwū　hái　méi　yǒu　huí　sùshè　ně!

My roommate has not yet returned to the dormitory.

16. 我　只　借了　画报,　没　有　借　小
Wǒ　zhǐ　jièlě　huàbào,　méi　yǒu　jiè　xiǎo-

说儿.
shuōr.

I borrowed only a picture news magazine, I did not
borrow a novel.

課文　Kèwén　Text

SIDE SIX, BAND SEVEN

(a₁)　昨天　是　星期日,　您　作　什么　了?
Zuótiǎn　shì　xīngqīrì,　nín　zuò　shénmǒ　lě?

Yesterday was Sunday; what did you (formal) do?

(b₁)　我　进　城　了.　我　看了　一个　朋友.
Wǒ　jìn　chéng　lě.　Wǒ　kànlě　yígě　péngyǒu.

I went into the city (into town). I saw a friend.

(a₂)　您的　这个　朋友　是　作　什么　工
Níndě　zhèigě　péngyǒu　shì　zuò　shénmǒ　gōng-

作　的,　您　能　告诉　我　吗?
zuò　dě,　nín　néng　gàosǔ　wǒ　mǎ?

Can you (formal) tell me what work this friend of
yours does?

(b₂)　他　在　学校里　教　书.
Tā　zài　xuéxiàolǐ　jiāo　shū.

He is a schoolteacher.

(a₃) 他　教　什么?
Tā　jiāo　shénmǒ?

What does he teach?

(b₃) 他　教　俄文.　我　朋友　教　俄文
Tā　jiāo　èwén.　Wǒ　péngyǒu　jiāo　èwén

的　方法　很　好,　学生　都　学得
dě　fāngfǎ　hěn　hǎo,　xuéshēng　dōu　xuédě

很　快.　他們　从　九月　起　开始
hěn　kuài.　Tāmēn　cóng　jiǔyuè　qǐ　kāishǐ

学習,　已經　会　説、会　写　了.
xuéxí,　yǐjīng　huì　shuō、huì　xiě　lě.

He teaches Russian. My friend's method of teaching
Russian is very good; his students learn very quickly.
They started to learn in September and can already
speak and write.

(a₄) 他們　每天　都　有　課　嗎?
Tāmēn　měitiān　dōu　yǒu　kè　mǎ?

Do they have classes every day?

(b₄) 都　有.　从　星期一　到　星期六
Dōu　yǒu.　Cóng　xīngqīyī　dào　xīngqīliù

他　每天　講　两节　語法.　你
tā　měitiān　jiǎng　liǎngjié　yǔfǎ.　Nǐ

星期日　进　城　了　嗎?
xīngqīrì　jìn　chéng　lě　mǎ?

Yes. Every day from Monday to Saturday he gives two
grammar lessons. Did you go into the city on Sunday?

(a₅) 没　有,　我　在　宿舍　看　書　了.
Méi　yǒu,　wǒ　zài　sùshè　kàn　shū　lě.

我　星期六　从　朋友　那兒　借了
Wǒ　xīngqīliù　cóng　péngyǒu　nàr　jièlě

一本　　翻譯　　小説兒,　星期日　一天
yìběn　　fānyì　　xiǎoshuōr,　xīngqīrì　yìtiān

我　都　看　小説兒　了.
wǒ　dōu　kàn　xiǎoshuōr　lê.

No, I read in the dormitory. On Saturday I borrowed a translated novel from a friend, and on Sunday (in one day) I read the whole novel.

(b₅)　这本　　小説兒　写得　怎么样?
Zhèiběn　xiǎoshuōr　xiědê　zěnmôyàng?

How is the writing in this novel?

(a₆)　这本　　小説兒　写得　很　好. 你　要
Zhèiběn　xiǎoshuōr　xiědê　hěn　hǎo.　Nǐ　yào

不　要　看?
bú　yào　kàn?

Very good. Do you want to read it?

(b₆)　我　要　看. 下星期　还,　可以　嗎?
Wǒ　yào　kàn.　Xiàxīngqī　huán,　kěyi　mǎ?

Yes. I'll return it next week. May I?

(a₇)　可以,　你　可以　慢慢兒地　看.
Kěyi,　nǐ　kěyi　mànmānrdê　kàn.

我　不　一定　现在　还　他.
Wǒ　bù　yídìng　xiànzài　huán　tā.

Yes. You may read it (very) slowly. I'm certainly not returning it to him now.

(b₇)　好.
Hǎo.

Good.

Vocabulary

(The words are arranged in the order of the phonetic alphabet, and the number after each word represents the number of the lesson in which the word appears.)

B

bā	八	(数)	bā	eight	22
bǎ	把	(量)	bǎ	(a measure word)	17
bàn	半	(数)	bàn	half	22
bāng	帮助	(动)	bāngzhù	to help	28
bào	报	(名)	bào	newspaper	13
běi	北京	(名)	Běijīng	Peking	14
	北京大学	(名)	Běijīng-dàxué	Peking University	17
běn	本	(量)	běn	(a measure word)	14
	本子	(名)	běnzi〔本〕	note-book	16
bì	必須	(能动)	bìxū	must, have to	29
bù	不	(副)	bù	not, no	13

C

chà	差	(动)	chà	less	25
cháng	長	(形)	cháng	long	15
	常常	(副)	chángcháng	often	21
chàng	唱（歌兒）	(动)	chàng(gēr)	to sing (song)	21
chéng	城	(名)	chéng	city, town	27
cí	詞彙	(名)	cíhuì	vocabulary	27

cóng	从	(介)	cóng	from	20
	从前	(副)	cóngqián	in the past, formerly	27
	从...起		cóng...qǐ	since, from the time of	28
	从...到...		cóng...dào...	from... to...	28

D

dà	大	(形)	dà	big, large	14
dē	的	(助)	dē	(a structural particle)	15
	地	(助)	dē	(a structural particle)	20
	得	(助)	dē	(a structural particle)	21
	...的时候儿		...dēshíhóur	when, at the time of	28
dì	地方	(名)	dìfāng	place	23
diǎn	点(鐘)	(名)	diǎn(zhōng)	o'clock	25
diàn	电影	(名)	diànyǐng	film, moving picture	20
dōng	东西	(名)	dōngxi	thing	26
dǒng	懂	(动)	dǒng	to understand, to know	19
dōu	都	(副)	dōu	all	17
duǎn	短	(形)	duǎn	short	15
duì	对了		duìlē	yes, that is right	17
	对	(形)	duì	right, correct	29
duō	多	(形)	duō	many, much	14
	多少	(数)	duōshǎo	how many, how much	22

E

| è | 俄文 | (名) | èwén | the Russian language | 15 |
| èr | 二 | (数) | èr | two | 22 |

F

| fān | 翻譯 | (动、名) | fānyì | to translate, to interpret translation, interpretation, interpreter | 28 |
| fāng | 方法 | (名) | fāngfǎ | way, method | 29 |

fēn	分	(名)	fēn	minute	25
fù	复習	(动)	fùxí	to review	27

G

gān	干淨	(形)	gānjing	clean	15
gāng	鋼笔	(名)	gāngbǐ 〔枝〕	pen	17
gāo	高兴	(形)	gāoxìng	glad, happy	20
gào	告訴	(动)	gàosù	to tell, to inform	29
gē	歌兒	(名)	gēr	song	21
gè	个	(量)	gè	(a measure word)	14
gěi	給	(动)	gěi	to give	16
gēn	跟	(介)	gēn	with, after	20
gōng	工作	(动、名)	gōngzuò	to work, work	16
	工厂	(名)	gōngchǎng	factory	23
guó	国	(名)	guó	country	19
guò	过	(动)	guò	to pass, past	25

H

hái	还	(副)	hái	also, too, still	26
	还是	(連)	háishì	or	29
hàn	汉字	(名)	hànzì	Chinese character	21
hǎo	好	(形)	hǎo	good, well	14
	好看	(形)	hǎokàn	good-looking	26
hào	号	(名)	hào	day, number	25
hé	和	(連)	hé	and	17
hēi	黑板	(名)	hēibǎn	blackboard	15
hěn	很	(副)	hěn	very	14
hòu	后边兒	(名)	hòubiānr	back, the following	23
huà	画报	(名)	huàbào 〔本〕	pictorial	17
	話	(名)	huà	words, speech	21

huán	还	(动)	huán	to return, to give back	29
huí	回	(动)	huí	to go back, to return	27
	回答	(动、名)	huídá	to answer, to reply	29
huì	会	(动)	huì	to know how to do	17
	会	(能动)	huì	can, may	26

J

ji	积极	(形)	jījí	enthusiastic, active	20
jǐ	几	(数)	jǐ	how many, several, a few	22
jiǎng	講	(动)	jiǎng	to explain, to give a lecture on, to tell	27
jiāo	教	(动)	jiāo	to teach	16
jiào	叫	(动)	jiào	to call, to be called	19
	教室	(名)	jiàoshì	classroom	28
jié	节	(量)	jié	(a measure word)	28
jiè	借	(动)	jiè	to lend, to borrow	29
jīn	今天	(名)	jīntiān	today	25
	今年	(名)	jīnnián	this year	25
jìn	进	(动)	jìn	to enter	27
jiù	旧	(形)	jiù	old	14
	就	(副)	jiù	then, at once	27
jù	句子	(名)	jùzi	sentence	27
jué	觉得	(动)	juédé	to feel	26

K

kāi	开始	(动)	kāishǐ	to start, to begin	28
kàn	看	(动)	kàn	to see, to look at	16
kě	可以	(能动)	kěyǐ	may	29
kè	刻	(名)	kè	a quarter	25
	課	(名)	kè	lesson, class	28
kuài	快	(形)	kuài	quick, fast	21

L

lái	来	(动)	lái	to come	16
lē	了	(尾、助)	lē	(a suffix and a particle)	27
lǐ	里边儿	(名)	lǐbiānr	inside	23
	礼堂	(名)	lǐtáng	auditorium (hall)	23
liàn	練習	(名、动)	liànxí	exercise, to exercise, to practise	22
liǎng	两	(数)	liǎng	two	22
liù	六	(数)	liù	six	22

M

mā	嗎	(助)	mā	(an interrogative particle)	13
mǎi	买	(动)	mǎi	to buy	26
màn	慢	(形)	màn	slow	21
máng	忙	(形)	máng	busy	25
méi	沒	(副)	méi	not	16
	沒关系		méiguānxì	never mind, it doesn't matter	26
měi	每	(代)	měi	each, every	29
míng	名字	(名)	míngzì	name	19
	明天	(名)	míngtiān	tomorrow	27

N

nǎ	哪兒	(代)	nǎr	where	20
	哪里	(代)	nǎlǐ	where	20
nà	那兒	(代)	nàr	there	20
	那里	(代)	nàlǐ	there	20
nē	呢	(助)	nē	(a particle)	27
něi	哪	(代)	něi	which	19
nèi	那	(代)	nèi, nà	that	13

néng	能	(能动)	néng	to be able, can	26
nǐ	你	(代)	nǐ	you	13
	你們	(代)	nǐměn	you	15
nián	年	(名)	nián	year	22
niàn	念	(动)	niàn	to read	21
nín	您	(代)	nín	(the polite form of 你)	13
nǔ	努力	(形)	nǔlì	diligent, strenuous	20

P

| páng | 旁边兒 | (名) | pángbiānr | side, beside | 23 |
| péng | 朋友 | (名) | péngyǒu | friend | 15 |

Q

qī	七	(数)	qī	seven	22
qiān	鉛笔	(名)	qiānbǐ 〔枝〕	pencil	15
qián	前边兒	(名)	qiánbiānr	front	23
qīng	清楚	(形)	qīngchǔ	clear	27
qù	去	(动)	qù	to go	20

R

rén	人	(名)	rén	man, person	13
	人民	(名)	rénmín	people	19
rèn	認識	(动、名)	rènshi	to know, to recognize	26
rì	日	(名)	rì	day	25

S

sān	三	(数)	sān	three	14
shàng	上边兒	(名)	shàngbiānr	above	23
	上(星期)		shàng(xīngqī)	last (week)	27
	上(課)		shàng(kè)	to go to class, to attend class	28
	上(月)		shàng(yuè)	last month, ultimo	28
shǎo	少	(形)	shǎo	few, little	14

shéi	誰	(代)	shéi	who	19
shén	什么	(代)	shénmǒ	what	19
shēng	生詞	(名)	shēngcí	new word	29
shí	十	(数)	shí	ten	22
	时候兒	(名)	shíhǒur	time	25
shì	是	(动)	shì	to be	13
shū	書	(名)	shū	book	13
shuō	說(話)	(动)	shuō(huà)	to speak	21
sì	四	(数)	sì	four	22
sū	苏联	(名)	Sūlián	the Soviet Union	19
sù	宿舍	(名)	sùshè	dormitory, hostel	23

T

tā	他	(代)	tā	he, him	13
	他們	(代)	tāměn	they, them	15
	她	(代)	tā	she, her	15
	它	(代)	tā	it	15
tài	太	(副)	tài	too	21
tè	特別	(形)	tèbié	special, particular	28
tiān	天	(名)	tiān	day	25
tiào	跳(舞)	(动)	tiào(wǔ)	to dance	21
tīng	听	(动)	tīng	to hear, to listen to	26
tóng	同志	(名)	tóngzhì	comrade	15
	同屋	(名)	tóngwū	room-mate	19
tú	圖書館	(名)	túshūguǎn	library	23

W

wài	外边儿	(名)	wàibiānr	outside	23
wǎn	晚	(形)	wǎn	late	21
wèn	問	(动)	wèn	to ask, to inquire	29
	問題	(名)	wèntí	question, problem	29
wǒ	我	(代)	wǒ	I, me	13
	我們	(代)	wǒměn	we, us	15
wǔ	五	(数)	wǔ	five	22

X

xĭ	喜欢	(动)	xĭhuån	to like, to be fond of	20
xià	下边兒	(名)	xiàbiånr	below, the following	23
	下(星期)		xià(xīngqi)	next (week)	27
	下(課)		xià(kè)	the class is over, after class	28
xiān	先生	(名)	xiānshěng	teacher, Mr., sir	13
xiàn	现在	(名)	xiànzài	now, at present	25
xiǎng	想	(动、能动)	xiǎng	to think, to want, to intend	29
xiǎo	小	(形)	xiǎo	little, small	14
	小說兒	(名)	xiǎoshuōr 〔本〕	novel	29
xiē	些	(量)	xiē	some	19
xiě	写	(动)	xiě	to write	21
xiè	謝謝		xièxiě	to thank, thanks	29
xīn	新	(形)	xīn	new	14
xīng	星期	(名)	xīngqī	week	25
xiū	休息	(动)	xiūxi	rest, to take a rest	28
xué	学生	(名)	xuéshěng	student	13
	学習	(动)	xuéxí	to study	16
	学	(动)	xué	to learn, to study	19
	学校	(名)	xuéxiào	school	20

Y

yào	要	(动、能动)	yào	to want, should	26
yě	也	(副)	yě	also, too	17
yī	一	(数)	yī	a, one	14
yí	一定	(副)	yídìng	certainly	21
yĭ	椅子	(名)	yĭzi 〔把〕	chair	17
	以后	(副)	yĭhòu	afterwards	26
	已經	(副)	yĭjīng	already	28

yì	一起	(副)	yìqǐ	together	20
yīng	应該	(能动)	yīnggāi	should, ought	26
yòng	用	(动)	yòng	to use	26
yǒu	有	(动)	yǒu	to have	16
	有意思		yǒuyìsi	interesting	17
yǔ	語法	(名)	yǔfǎ	grammar	27
yuè	月	(名)	yuè	month	25

Z

zá	杂誌	(名)	zázhì 〔本〕	magazine	17
zài	在	(动)	zài	to be, on, in, at	23
zǎo	早	(形)	zǎo	early	21
zěn	怎么样	(代)	zěnmǒyàng	how (is it)	19
zhāng	張	(量)	zhāng	(a measure word)	14
zhè	这兒	(代)	zhèr	here	20
	这里	(代)	zhèli	here	20
zhèi	这	(代)	zhèi, zhè	this	13
zhī	枝	(量)	zhī	(a measure word)	15
	知道	(动)	zhīdǎo	to know	19
zhǐ	紙	(名)	zhǐ 〔張〕	paper	14
	只	(副)	zhǐ	only	16
zhōng	中国	(名)	Zhōngguó	China, Chinese	13
	中文	(名)	zhōngwén	the Chinese language	16
	中间兒	(名)	zhōngjiànr	middle	23
zhù	住	(动)	zhù	to live, to dwell	28
zhuō	桌子	(名)	zhuōzi 〔張〕	table	17
zì	字典	(名)	zìdiǎn	dictionary	26
	字	(名)	zì	character	28
zuó	昨天	(名)	zuótiān	yesterday	27
zuò	作	(动)	zuò	to do, to make, to work, to be	23

A CATALOG OF SELECTED
DOVER BOOKS
IN ALL FIELDS OF INTEREST

A CATALOG OF SELECTED DOVER
BOOKS IN ALL FIELDS OF INTEREST

CONCERNING THE SPIRITUAL IN ART, Wassily Kandinsky. Pioneering work by father of abstract art. Thoughts on color theory, nature of art. Analysis of earlier masters. 12 illustrations. 80pp. of text. 5⅜ × 8½. 23411-8 Pa. $2.50

LEONARDO ON THE HUMAN BODY, Leonardo da Vinci. More than 1200 of Leonardo's anatomical drawings on 215 plates. Leonardo's text, which accompanies the drawings, has been translated into English. 506pp. 8⅜ × 11¼. 24483-0 Pa. $10.95

GOBLIN MARKET, Christina Rossetti. Best-known work by poet comparable to Emily Dickinson, Alfred Tennyson. With 46 delightfully grotesque illustrations by Laurence Housman. 64pp. 4 × 6¼. 24516-0 Pa. $2.50

THE HEART OF THOREAU'S JOURNALS, edited by Odell Shepard. Selections from *Journal*, ranging over full gamut of interests. 228pp. 5⅜ × 8½. 20741-2 Pa. $4.50

MR. LINCOLN'S CAMERA MAN: MATHEW B. BRADY, Roy Meredith. Over 300 Brady photos reproduced directly from original negatives, photos. Lively commentary. 368pp. 8⅜ × 11¼. 23021-X Pa. $14.95

PHOTOGRAPHIC VIEWS OF SHERMAN'S CAMPAIGN, George N. Barnard. Reprint of landmark 1866 volume with 61 plates: battlefield of New Hope Church, the Etawah Bridge, the capture of Atlanta, etc. 80pp. 9 × 12. 23445-2 Pa. $6.00

A SHORT HISTORY OF ANATOMY AND PHYSIOLOGY FROM THE GREEKS TO HARVEY, Dr. Charles Singer. Thoroughly engrossing non-technical survey. 270 illustrations. 211pp. 5⅜ × 8½. 20389-1 Pa. $4.95

REDOUTE ROSES IRON-ON TRANSFER PATTERNS, Barbara Christopher. Redouté was botanical painter to the Empress Josephine; transfer his famous roses onto fabric with these 24 transfer patterns. 80pp. 8¼ × 10⅞. 24292-7 Pa. $3.50

THE FIVE BOOKS OF ARCHITECTURE, Sebastiano Serlio. Architectural milestone, first (1611) English translation of Renaissance classic. Unabridged reproduction of original edition includes over 300 woodcut illustrations. 416pp. 9⅜ × 12¼. 24349-4 Pa. $14.95

CARLSON'S GUIDE TO LANDSCAPE PAINTING, John F. Carlson. Authoritative, comprehensive guide covers, every aspect of landscape painting. 34 reproductions of paintings by author; 58 explanatory diagrams. 144pp. 8⅜ × 11. 22927-0 Pa. $5.95

101 PUZZLES IN THOUGHT AND LOGIC, C.R. Wylie, Jr. Solve murders, robberies, see which fishermen are liars—purely by reasoning! 107pp. 5⅜ × 8½. 20367-0 Pa. $2.00

TEST YOUR LOGIC, George J. Summers. 50 more truly new puzzles with new turns of thought, new subtleties of inference. 100pp. 5⅜ × 8½. 22877-0 Pa. $2.25

25 KITES THAT FLY, Leslie Hunt. Full, easy-to-follow instructions for kites made from inexpensive materials. Many novelties. 70 illustrations. 110pp. 5⅜ × 8½.
22550-X Pa. $2.25

PIANO TUNING, J. Cree Fischer. Clearest, best book for beginner, amateur. Simple repairs, raising dropped notes, tuning by easy method of flattened fifths. No previous skills needed. 4 illustrations. 201pp. 5⅜ × 8½. 23267-0 Pa. $3.50

EARLY AMERICAN IRON-ON TRANSFER PATTERNS, edited by Rita Weiss. 75 designs, borders, alphabets, from traditional American sources. 48pp. 8¼ × 11.
23162-3 Pa. $1.95

CROCHETING EDGINGS, edited by Rita Weiss. Over 100 of the best designs for these lovely trims for a host of household items. Complete instructions, illustrations. 48pp. 8¼ × 11. 24031-2 Pa. $2.25

FINGER PLAYS FOR NURSERY AND KINDERGARTEN, Emilie Poulsson. 18 finger plays with music (voice and piano); entertaining, instructive. Counting, nature lore, etc. Victorian classic. 53 illustrations. 80pp. 6½ × 9¼. 22588-7 Pa. $1.95

BOSTON THEN AND NOW, Peter Vanderwarker. Here in 59 side-by-side views are photographic documentations of the city's past and present. 119 photographs. Full captions. 122pp. 8¼ × 11. 24312-5 Pa. $6.95

CROCHETING BEDSPREADS, edited by Rita Weiss. 22 patterns, originally published in three instruction books 1939-41. 39 photos, 8 charts. Instructions. 48pp. 8¼ × 11. 23610-2 Pa. $2.00

HAWTHORNE ON PAINTING, Charles W. Hawthorne. Collected from notes taken by students at famous Cape Cod School; hundreds of direct, personal *apercus*, ideas, suggestions. 91pp. 5⅜ × 8½. 20653-X Pa. $2.50

THERMODYNAMICS, Enrico Fermi. A classic of modern science. Clear, organized treatment of systems, first and second laws, entropy, thermodynamic potentials, etc. Calculus required. 160pp. 5⅜ × 8½. 60361-X Pa. $4.00

TEN BOOKS ON ARCHITECTURE, Vitruvius. The most important book ever written on architecture. Early Roman aesthetics, technology, classical orders, site selection, all other aspects. Morgan translation. 331pp. 5⅜ × 8½. 20645-9 Pa. $5.50

THE CORNELL BREAD BOOK, Clive M. McCay and Jeanette B. McCay. Famed high-protein recipe incorporated into breads, rolls, buns, coffee cakes, pizza, pie crusts, more. Nearly 50 illustrations. 48pp. 8¼ × 11. 23995-0 Pa. $2.00

THE CRAFTSMAN'S HANDBOOK, Cennino Cennini. 15th-century handbook, school of Giotto, explains applying gold, silver leaf; gesso; fresco painting, grinding pigments, etc. 142pp. 6⅛ × 9¼. 20054-X Pa. $3.50

FRANK LLOYD WRIGHT'S FALLINGWATER, Donald Hoffmann. Full story of Wright's masterwork at Bear Run, Pa. 100 photographs of site, construction, and details of completed structure. 112pp. 9¼ × 10. 23671-4 Pa. $6.95

OVAL STAINED GLASS PATTERN BOOK, C. Eaton. 60 new designs framed in shape of an oval. Greater complexity, challenge with sinuous cats, birds, mandalas framed in antique shape. 64pp. 8¼ × 11. 24519-5 Pa. $3.50

CHILDREN'S BOOKPLATES AND LABELS, Ed Sibbett, Jr. 6 each of 12 types based on *Wizard of Oz, Alice,* nursery rhymes, fairy tales. Perforated; full color. 24pp. 8¼ × 11. 23538-6 Pa. $3.50

READY-TO-USE VICTORIAN COLOR STICKERS: 96 Pressure-Sensitive Seals, Carol Belanger Grafton. Drawn from authentic period sources. Motifs include heads of men, women, children, plus florals, animals, birds, more. Will adhere to any clean surface. 8pp. 8½ × 11. 24551-9 Pa. $2.95

CUT AND FOLD PAPER SPACESHIPS THAT FLY, Michael Grater. 16 colorful, easy-to-build spaceships that really fly. Star Shuttle, Lunar Freighter, Star Probe, 13 others. 32pp. 8¼ × 11. 23978-0 Pa. $2.50

CUT AND ASSEMBLE PAPER AIRPLANES THAT FLY, Arthur Baker. 8 aerodynamically sound, ready-to-build paper airplanes, designed with latest techniques. Fly *Pegasus, Daedalus, Songbird,* 5 other aircraft. Instructions. 32pp. 9¼ × 11¼. 24302-8 Pa. $3.95

SIDELIGHTS ON RELATIVITY, Albert Einstein. Two lectures delivered in 1920-21: *Ether and Relativity* and *Geometry and Experience.* Elegant ideas in non-mathematical form. 56pp. 5⅜ × 8½. 24511-X Pa. $2.25

FADS AND FALLACIES IN THE NAME OF SCIENCE, Martin Gardner. Fair, witty appraisal of cranks and quacks of science: Velikovsky, orgone energy, Bridey Murphy, medical fads, etc. 373pp. 5⅜ × 8½. 20394-8 Pa. $5.95

VACATION HOMES AND CABINS, U.S. Dept. of Agriculture. Complete plans for 16 cabins, vacation homes and other shelters. 105pp. 9 × 12. 23631-5 Pa. $4.95

HOW TO BUILD A WOOD-FRAME HOUSE, L.O. Anderson. Placement, foundations, framing, sheathing, roof, insulation, plaster, finishing—almost everything else. 179 illustrations. 223pp. 7⅞ × 10¾. 22954-8 Pa. $5.50

THE MYSTERY OF A HANSOM CAB, Fergus W. Hume. Bizarre murder in a hansom cab leads to engrossing investigation. Memorable characters, rich atmosphere. 19th-century bestseller, still enjoyable, exciting. 256pp. 5⅜ × 8. 21956-9 Pa. $4.00

MANUAL OF TRADITIONAL WOOD CARVING, edited by Paul N. Hasluck. Possibly the best book in English on the craft of wood carving. Practical instructions, along with 1,146 working drawings and photographic illustrations. 576pp. 6½ × 9¼. 23489-4 Pa. $8.95

WHITTLING AND WOODCARVING, E.J Tangerman. Best book on market; clear, full. If you can cut a potato, you can carve toys, puzzles, chains, etc. Over 464 illustrations. 293pp. 5⅜ × 8½. 20965-2 Pa. $4.95

AMERICAN TRADEMARK DESIGNS, Barbara Baer Capitman. 732 marks, logos and corporate-identity symbols. Categories include entertainment, heavy industry, food and beverage. All black-and-white in standard forms. 160pp. 8⅛ × 11. 23259-X Pa. $6.95

DECORATIVE FRAMES AND BORDERS, edited by Edmund V. Gillon, Jr. Largest collection of borders and frames ever compiled for use of artists and designers. Renaissance, neo-Greek, Art Nouveau, Art Deco, to mention only a few styles. 396 illustrations. 192pp. 8⅜ × 11¼. 22928-9 Pa. $6.00

THE MURDER BOOK OF J.G. REEDER, Edgar Wallace. Eight suspenseful stories by bestselling mystery writer of 20s and 30s. Features the donnish Mr. J.G. Reeder of Public Prosecutor's Office. 128pp. 5⅜ × 8½. (Available in U.S. only)
24374-5 Pa. $3.50

ANNE ORR'S CHARTED DESIGNS, Anne Orr. Best designs by premier needlework designer, all on charts: flowers, borders, birds, children, alphabets, etc. Over 100 charts, 10 in color. Total of 40pp. 8¼ × 11.
23704-4 Pa. $2.50

BASIC CONSTRUCTION TECHNIQUES FOR HOUSES AND SMALL BUILDINGS SIMPLY EXPLAINED, U.S. Bureau of Naval Personnel. Grading, masonry, woodworking, floor and wall framing, roof framing, plastering, tile setting, much more. Over 675 illustrations. 568pp. 6½ × 9¼.
20242-9 Pa. $8.95

MATISSE LINE DRAWINGS AND PRINTS, Henri Matisse. Representative collection of female nudes, faces, still lifes, experimental works, etc., from 1898 to 1948. 50 illustrations. 48pp. 8⅜ × 11¼.
23877-6 Pa. $2.50

HOW TO PLAY THE CHESS OPENINGS, Eugene Znosko-Borovsky. Clear, profound examinations of just what each opening is intended to do and how opponent can counter. Many sample games. 147pp. 5⅜ × 8½.
22795-2 Pa. $2.95

DUPLICATE BRIDGE, Alfred Sheinwold. Clear, thorough, easily followed account: rules, etiquette, scoring, strategy, bidding; Goren's point-count system, Blackwood and Gerber conventions, etc. 158pp. 5⅜ × 8½.
22741-3 Pa. $3.00

SARGENT PORTRAIT DRAWINGS, J.S. Sargent. Collection of 42 portraits reveals technical skill and intuitive eye of noted American portrait painter, John Singer Sargent. 48pp. 8¼ × 11⅛.
24524-1 Pa. $2.95

ENTERTAINING SCIENCE EXPERIMENTS WITH EVERYDAY OBJECTS, Martin Gardner. Over 100 experiments for youngsters. Will amuse, astonish, teach, and entertain. Over 100 illustrations. 127pp. 5⅜ × 8½.
24201-3 Pa. $2.50

TEDDY BEAR PAPER DOLLS IN FULL COLOR: A Family of Four Bears and Their Costumes, Crystal Collins. A family of four Teddy Bear paper dolls and nearly 60 cut-out costumes. Full color, printed one side only. 32pp. 9¼ × 12¼.
24550-0 Pa. $3.50

NEW CALLIGRAPHIC ORNAMENTS AND FLOURISHES, Arthur Baker. Unusual, multi-useable material: arrows, pointing hands, brackets and frames, ovals, swirls, birds, etc. Nearly 700 illustrations. 80pp. 8⅜ × 11¼.
24095-9 Pa. $3.75

DINOSAUR DIORAMAS TO CUT & ASSEMBLE, M. Kalmenoff. Two complete three-dimensional scenes in full color, with 31 cut-out animals and plants. Excellent educational toy for youngsters. Instructions; 2 assembly diagrams. 32pp. 9¼ × 12¼.
24541-1 Pa. $4.50

SILHOUETTES: A PICTORIAL ARCHIVE OF VARIED ILLUSTRATIONS, edited by Carol Belanger Grafton. Over 600 silhouettes from the 18th to 20th centuries. Profiles and full figures of men, women, children, birds, animals, groups and scenes, nature, ships, an alphabet. 144pp. 8⅜ × 11¼.
23781-8 Pa. $4.95

THE BOOK OF WOOD CARVING, Charles Marshall Sayers. Still finest book for beginning student. Fundamentals, technique; gives 34 designs, over 34 projects for panels, bookends, mirrors, etc. 33 photos. 118pp. 7¾ × 10⅝. 23654-4 Pa. $3.95

CARVING COUNTRY CHARACTERS, Bill Higginbotham. Expert advice for beginning, advanced carvers on materials, techniques for creating 18 projects—mirthful panorama of American characters. 105 illustrations. 80pp. 8⅜ × 11. 24135-1 Pa. $2.50

300 ART NOUVEAU DESIGNS AND MOTIFS IN FULL COLOR, C.B. Grafton. 44 full-page plates display swirling lines and muted colors typical of Art Nouveau. Borders, frames, panels, cartouches, dingbats, etc. 48pp. 9⅜ × 12¼. 24354-0 Pa. $6.95

SELF-WORKING CARD TRICKS, Karl Fulves. Editor of *Pallbearer* offers 72 tricks that work automatically through nature of card deck. No sleight of hand needed. Often spectacular. 42 illustrations. 113pp. 5⅜ × 8½. 23334-0 Pa. $3.50

CUT AND ASSEMBLE A WESTERN FRONTIER TOWN, Edmund V. Gillon, Jr. Ten authentic full-color buildings on heavy cardboard stock in H-O scale. Sheriff's Office and Jail, Saloon, Wells Fargo, Opera House, others. 48pp. 9¼ × 12¼. 23736-2 Pa. $3.95

CUT AND ASSEMBLE AN EARLY NEW ENGLAND VILLAGE, Edmund V. Gillon, Jr. Printed in full color on heavy cardboard stock. 12 authentic buildings in H-O scale: Adams home in Quincy, Mass., Oliver Wight house in Sturbridge, smithy, store, church, others. 48pp. 9¼ × 12¼. 23536-X Pa. $4.95

THE TALE OF TWO BAD MICE, Beatrix Potter. Tom Thumb and Hunca Munca squeeze out of their hole and go exploring. 27 full-color Potter illustrations. 59pp. 4¼ × 5½. (Available in U.S. only) 23065-1 Pa. $1.75

CARVING FIGURE CARICATURES IN THE OZARK STYLE, Harold L. Enlow. Instructions and illustrations for ten delightful projects, plus general carving instructions. 22 drawings and 47 photographs altogether. 39pp. 8⅜ × 11. 23151-8 Pa. $2.50

A TREASURY OF FLOWER DESIGNS FOR ARTISTS, EMBROIDERERS AND CRAFTSMEN, Susan Gaber. 100 garden favorites lushly rendered by artist for artists, craftsmen, needleworkers. Many form frames, borders. 80pp. 8¼ × 11. 24096-7 Pa. $3.50

CUT & ASSEMBLE A TOY THEATER/THE NUTCRACKER BALLET, Tom Tierney. Model of a complete, full-color production of Tchaikovsky's classic. 6 backdrops, dozens of characters, familiar dance sequences. 32pp. 9⅜ × 12¼. 24194-7 Pa. $4.50

ANIMALS: 1,419 COPYRIGHT-FREE ILLUSTRATIONS OF MAMMALS, BIRDS, FISH, INSECTS, ETC., edited by Jim Harter. Clear wood engravings present, in extremely lifelike poses, over 1,000 species of animals. 284pp. 9 × 12. 23766-4 Pa. $9.95

MORE HAND SHADOWS, Henry Bursill. For those at their 'finger ends," 16 more effects—Shakespeare, a hare, a squirrel, Mr. Punch, and twelve more—each explained by a full-page illustration. Considerable period charm. 30pp. 6½ × 9¼. 21384-6 Pa. $1.95

JAPANESE DESIGN MOTIFS, Matsuya Co. Mon, or heraldic designs. Over 4000 typical, beautiful designs: birds, animals, flowers, swords, fans, geometrics; all beautifully stylized. 213pp. 11⅜ × 8¼. 22874-6 Pa. $7.95

THE TALE OF BENJAMIN BUNNY, Beatrix Potter. Peter Rabbit's cousin coaxes him back into Mr. McGregor's garden for a whole new set of adventures. All 27 full-color illustrations. 59pp. 4¼ × 5½. (Available in U.S. only) 21102-9 Pa. $1.75

THE TALE OF PETER RABBIT AND OTHER FAVORITE STORIES BOXED SET, Beatrix Potter. Seven of Beatrix Potter's best-loved tales including Peter Rabbit in a specially designed, durable boxed set. 4¼ × 5½. Total of 447pp. 158 color illustrations. (Available in U.S. only) 23903-9 Pa. $10.80

PRACTICAL MENTAL MAGIC, Theodore Annemann. Nearly 200 astonishing feats of mental magic revealed in step-by-step detail. Complete advice on staging, patter, etc. Illustrated. 320pp. 5⅜ × 8½. 24426-1 Pa. $5.95

CELEBRATED CASES OF JUDGE DEE (DEE GOONG AN), translated by Robert Van Gulik. Authentic 18th-century Chinese detective novel; Dee and associates solve three interlocked cases. Led to van Gulik's own stories with same characters. Extensive introduction. 9 illustrations. 237pp. 5⅜ × 8½. 23337-5 Pa. $4.50

CUT & FOLD EXTRATERRESTRIAL INVADERS THAT FLY, M. Grater. Stage your own lilliputian space battles.By following the step-by-step instructions and explanatory diagrams you can launch 22 full-color fliers into space. 36pp. 8¼ × 11. 24478-4 Pa. $2.95

CUT & ASSEMBLE VICTORIAN HOUSES, Edmund V. Gillon, Jr. Printed in full color on heavy cardboard stock, 4 authentic Victorian houses in H-O scale: Italian-style Villa, Octagon, Second Empire, Stick Style. 48pp. 9¼ × 12¼. 23849-0 Pa. $3.95

BEST SCIENCE FICTION STORIES OF H.G. WELLS, H.G. Wells. Full novel *The Invisible Man,* plus 17 short stories: "The Crystal Egg," "Aepyornis Island," "The Strange Orchid," etc. 303pp. 5⅜ × 8½. (Available in U.S. only) 21531-8 Pa. $4.95

TRADEMARK DESIGNS OF THE WORLD, Yusaku Kamekura. A lavish collection of nearly 700 trademarks, the work of Wright, Loewy, Klee, Binder, hundreds of others. 160pp. 8¾ × 8. (Available in U.S. only) 24191-2 Pa. $5.95

THE ARTIST'S AND CRAFTSMAN'S GUIDE TO REDUCING, ENLARGING AND TRANSFERRING DESIGNS, Rita Weiss. Discover, reduce, enlarge, transfer designs from any objects to any craft project. 12pp. plus 16 sheets special graph paper. 8¼ × 11. 24142-4 Pa. $3.50

TREASURY OF JAPANESE DESIGNS AND MOTIFS FOR ARTISTS AND CRAFTSMEN, edited by Carol Belanger Grafton. Indispensable collection of 360 traditional Japanese designs and motifs redrawn in clean, crisp black-and-white, copyright-free illustrations. 96pp. 8¼ × 11. 24435-0 Pa. $3.95

TWENTY-FOUR ART NOUVEAU POSTCARDS IN FULL COLOR FROM CLASSIC POSTERS, Hayward and Blanche Cirker. Ready-to-mail postcards reproduced from rare set of poster art. Works by Toulouse-Lautrec, Parrish, Steinlen, Mucha, Cheret, others. 12pp. 8¼× 11.   24389-3 Pa. $2.95

READY-TO-USE ART NOUVEAU BOOKMARKS IN FULL COLOR, Carol Belanger Grafton. 30 elegant bookmarks featuring graceful, flowing lines, foliate motifs, sensuous women characteristic of Art Nouveau. Perforated for easy detaching. 16pp. 8¼ × 11.   24305-2 Pa. $2.95

FRUIT KEY AND TWIG KEY TO TREES AND SHRUBS, William M. Harlow. Fruit key covers 120 deciduous and evergreen species; twig key covers 160 deciduous species. Easily used. Over 300 photographs. 126pp. 5⅜ × 8½.   20511-8 Pa. $2.25

LEONARDO DRAWINGS, Leonardo da Vinci. Plants, landscapes, human face and figure, etc., plus studies for Sforza monument, *Last Supper*, more. 60 illustrations. 64pp. 8¼ × 11⅛.   23951-9 Pa. $2.75

CLASSIC BASEBALL CARDS, edited by Bert R. Sugar. 98 classic cards on heavy stock, full color, perforated for detaching. Ruth, Cobb, Durocher, DiMaggio, H. Wagner, 99 others. Rare originals cost hundreds. 16pp. 8¼ × 11. 23498-3 Pa. $3.25

TREES OF THE EASTERN AND CENTRAL UNITED STATES AND CANADA, William M. Harlow. Best one-volume guide to 140 trees. Full descriptions, woodlore, range, etc. Over 600 illustrations. Handy size. 288pp. 4½ × 6⅜.   20395-6 Pa. $3.95

JUDY GARLAND PAPER DOLLS IN FULL COLOR, Tom Tierney. 3 Judy Garland paper dolls (teenager, grown-up, and mature woman) and 30 gorgeous costumes highlighting memorable career. Captions. 32pp. 9¼ × 12¼.
24404-0 Pa. $3.50

GREAT FASHION DESIGNS OF THE BELLE EPOQUE PAPER DOLLS IN FULL COLOR, Tom Tierney. Two dolls and 30 costumes meticulously rendered. Haute couture by Worth, Lanvin, Paquin, other greats late Victorian to WWI. 32pp. 9¼ × 12¼.   24425-3 Pa. $3.50

FASHION PAPER DOLLS FROM GODEY'S LADY'S BOOK, 1840-1854, Susan Johnston. In full color: 7 female fashion dolls with 50 costumes. Little girl's, bridal, riding, bathing, wedding, evening, everyday, etc. 32pp. 9¼ × 12¼.
23511-4 Pa. $3.95

THE BOOK OF THE SACRED MAGIC OF ABRAMELIN THE MAGE, translated by S. MacGregor Mathers. Medieval manuscript of ceremonial magic. Basic document in Aleister Crowley, Golden Dawn groups. 268pp. 5⅜ × 8½.
23211-5 Pa. $5.00

PETER RABBIT POSTCARDS IN FULL COLOR: 24 Ready-to-Mail Cards, Susan Whited LaBelle. Bunnies ice-skating, coloring Easter eggs, making valentines, many other charming scenes. 24 perforated full-color postcards, each measuring 4¼ × 6, on coated stock. 12pp. 9 × 12.   24617-5 Pa. $2.95

CELTIC HAND STROKE BY STROKE, A. Baker. Complete guide creating each letter of the alphabet in distinctive Celtic manner. Covers hand position, strokes, pens, inks, paper, more. Illustrated. 48pp. 8¼ × 11.   24336-2 Pa. $2.50

HOW THE OTHER HALF LIVES, Jacob A. Riis. Journalistic record of filth, degradation, upward drive in New York immigrant slums, shops, around 1900. New edition includes 100 original Riis photos, monuments of early photography. 233pp. 10 × 7⅞. 22012-5 Pa. $7.95

CHINA AND ITS PEOPLE IN EARLY PHOTOGRAPHS, John Thomson. In 200 black-and-white photographs of exceptional quality photographic pioneer Thomson captures the mountains, dwellings, monuments and people of 19th-century China. 272pp. 9⅜ × 12¼. 24393-1 Pa. $12.95

GODEY COSTUME PLATES IN COLOR FOR DECOUPAGE AND FRAMING, edited by Eleanor Hasbrouk Rawlings. 24 full-color engravings depicting 19th-century Parisian haute couture. Printed on one side only. 56pp. 8¼ × 11. 23879-2 Pa. $3.95

ART NOUVEAU STAINED GLASS PATTERN BOOK, Ed Sibbett, Jr. 104 projects using well-known themes of Art Nouveau: swirling forms, florals, peacocks, and sensuous women. 60pp. 8¼ × 11. 23577-7 Pa. $3.50

QUICK AND EASY PATCHWORK ON THE SEWING MACHINE: Susan Aylsworth Murwin and Suzzy Payne. Instructions, diagrams show exactly how to machine sew 12 quilts. 48pp. of templates. 50 figures. 80pp. 8¼ × 11. 23770-2 Pa. $3.50

THE STANDARD BOOK OF QUILT MAKING AND COLLECTING, Marguerite Ickis. Full information, full-sized patterns for making 46 traditional quilts, also 150 other patterns. 483 illustrations. 273pp. 6⅞ × 9⅝. 20582-7 Pa. $5.95

LETTERING AND ALPHABETS, J. Albert Cavanagh. 85 complete alphabets lettered in various styles; instructions for spacing, roughs, brushwork. 121pp. 8¾ × 8. 20053-1 Pa. $3.95

LETTER FORMS: 110 COMPLETE ALPHABETS, Frederick Lambert. 110 sets of capital letters; 16 lower case alphabets; 70 sets of numbers and other symbols. 110pp. 8⅛ × 11. 22872-X Pa. $4.50

ORCHIDS AS HOUSE PLANTS, Rebecca Tyson Northen. Grow cattleyas and many other kinds of orchids—in a window, in a case, or under artificial light. 63 illustrations. 148pp. 5⅜ × 8½. 23261-1 Pa. $2.95

THE MUSHROOM HANDBOOK, Louis C.C. Krieger. Still the best popular handbook. Full descriptions of 259 species, extremely thorough text, poisons, folklore, etc. 32 color plates; 126 other illustrations. 560pp. 5⅜ × 8½. 21861-9 Pa. $8.50

THE DORÉ BIBLE ILLUSTRATIONS, Gustave Doré. All wonderful, detailed plates: Adam and Eve, Flood, Babylon, life of Jesus, etc. Brief King James text with each plate. 241 plates. 241pp. 9 × 12. 23004-X Pa. $8.95

THE BOOK OF KELLS: Selected Plates in Full Color, edited by Blanche Cirker. 32 full-page plates from greatest manuscript-icon of early Middle Ages. Fantastic, mysterious. Publisher's Note. Captions. 32pp. 9¾ × 12¼. 24345-1 Pa. $4.50

THE PERFECT WAGNERITE, George Bernard Shaw. Brilliant criticism of the Ring Cycle, with provocative interpretation of politics, economic theories behind the Ring. 136pp. 5⅜ × 8½. (Available in U.S. only) 21707-8 Pa. $3.00

CATALOG OF DOVER BOOKS

REASON IN ART, George Santayana. Renowned philosopher's provocative, seminal treatment of basis of art in instinct and experience. Volume Four of *The Life of Reason*. 230pp. 5⅜ × 8.   24358-3 Pa. $4.50

LANGUAGE, TRUTH AND LOGIC, Alfred J. Ayer. Famous, clear introduction to Vienna, Cambridge schools of Logical Positivism. Role of philosophy, elimination of metaphysics, nature of analysis, etc. 160pp. 5⅜ × 8½. (USCO)
20010-8 Pa. $2.75

BASIC ELECTRONICS, U.S. Bureau of Naval Personnel. Electron tubes, circuits, antennas, AM, FM, and CW transmission and receiving, etc. 560 illustrations. 567pp. 6½ × 9¼.   21076-6 Pa. $8.95

THE ART DECO STYLE, edited by Theodore Menten. Furniture, jewelry, metalwork, ceramics, fabrics, lighting fixtures, interior decors, exteriors, graphics from pure French sources. Over 400 photographs. 183pp. 8⅜ × 11¼.
22824-X Pa. $6.95

THE FOUR BOOKS OF ARCHITECTURE, Andrea Palladio. 16th-century classic covers classical architectural remains, Renaissance revivals, classical orders, etc. 1738 Ware English edition. 216 plates. 110pp. of text. 9½ × 12¾.
21308-0 Pa. $11.50

THE WIT AND HUMOR OF OSCAR WILDE, edited by Alvin Redman. More than 1000 ripostes, paradoxes, wisecracks: Work is the curse of the drinking classes, I can resist everything except temptations, etc. 258pp. 5⅜ × 8½. (USCO)
20602-5 Pa. $3.95

THE DEVIL'S DICTIONARY, Ambrose Bierce. Barbed, bitter, brilliant witticisms in the form of a dictionary. Best, most ferocious satire America has produced. 145pp. 5⅜ × 8½.   20487-1 Pa. $2.50

ERTÉ'S FASHION DESIGNS, Erté. 210 black-and-white inventions from *Harper's Bazar*, 1918-32, plus 8pp. full-color covers. Captions. 88pp. 9 × 12.
24203-X Pa. $6.50

ERTÉ GRAPHICS, Erté. Collection of striking color graphics: *Seasons, Alphabet, Numerals, Aces* and *Precious Stones*. 50 plates, including 4 on covers. 48pp. 9⅜ × 12¼.   23580-7 Pa. $6.95

PAPER FOLDING FOR BEGINNERS, William D. Murray and Francis J. Rigney. Clearest book for making origami sail boats, roosters, frogs that move legs, etc. 40 projects. More than 275 illustrations. 94pp. 5⅜ × 8½.   20713-7 Pa. $2.25

ORIGAMI FOR THE ENTHUSIAST, John Montroll. Fish, ostrich, peacock, squirrel, rhinoceros, Pegasus, 19 other intricate subjects. Instructions. Diagrams. 128pp. 9 × 12.   23799-0 Pa. $4.95

CROCHETING NOVELTY POT HOLDERS, edited by Linda Macho. 64 useful, whimsical pot holders feature kitchen themes, animals, flowers, other novelties. Surprisingly easy to crochet. Complete instructions. 48pp. 8¼ × 11.
24296-X Pa. $1.95

CROCHETING DOILIES, edited by Rita Weiss. Irish Crochet, Jewel, Star Wheel, Vanity Fair and more. Also luncheon and console sets, runners and centerpieces. 51 illustrations. 48pp. 8¼ × 11.   23424-X Pa. $2.50

YUCATAN BEFORE AND AFTER THE CONQUEST, Diego de Landa. Only significant account of Yucatan written in the early post-Conquest era. Translated by William Gates. Over 120 illustrations. 162pp. 5⅜ × 8½.   23622-6 Pa. $3.50

ORNATE PICTORIAL CALLIGRAPHY, E.A. Lupfer. Complete instructions, over 150 examples help you create magnificent "flourishes" from which beautiful animals and objects gracefully emerge. 8⅛ × 11.   21957-7 Pa. $2.95

DOLLY DINGLE PAPER DOLLS, Grace Drayton. Cute chubby children by same artist who did Campbell Kids. Rare plates from 1910s. 30 paper dolls and over 100 outfits reproduced in full color. 32pp. 9¼ × 12¼.   23711-7 Pa. $3.50

CURIOUS GEORGE PAPER DOLLS IN FULL COLOR, H. A. Rey, Kathy Allert. Naughty little monkey-hero of children's books in two doll figures, plus 48 full-color costumes: pirate, Indian chief, fireman, more. 32pp. 9¼ × 12¼.
23386-9 Pa. $3.50

GERMAN: HOW TO SPEAK AND WRITE IT, Joseph Rosenberg. Like *French, How to Speak and Write It*. Very rich modern course, with a wealth of pictorial material. 330 illustrations. 384pp. 5⅜ × 8½. (USUKO)   20271-2 Pa. $4.75

CATS AND KITTENS: 24 Ready-to-Mail Color Photo Postcards, D. Holby. Handsome collection; feline in a variety of adorable poses. Identifications. 12pp. on postcard stock. 8¼ × 11.   24469-5 Pa. $2.95

MARILYN MONROE PAPER DOLLS, Tom Tierney. 31 full-color designs on heavy stock, from *The Asphalt Jungle, Gentlemen Prefer Blondes*, 22 others.1 doll. 16 plates. 32pp. 9⅜ × 12¼.   23769-9 Pa. $3.50

FUNDAMENTALS OF LAYOUT, F.H. Wills. All phases of layout design discussed and illustrated in 121 illustrations. Indispensable as student's text or handbook for professional. 124pp. 8⅜ × 11.   21279-3 Pa. $4.50

FANTASTIC SUPER STICKERS, Ed Sibbett, Jr. 75 colorful pressure-sensitive stickers. Peel off and place for a touch of pizzazz: clowns, penguins, teddy bears, etc. Full color. 16pp. 8¼ × 11.   24471-7 Pa. $2.95

LABELS FOR ALL OCCASIONS, Ed Sibbett, Jr. 6 labels each of 16 different designs—baroque, art nouveau, art deco, Pennsylvania Dutch, etc.—in full color. 24pp. 8¼ × 11.   23688-9 Pa. $2.95

HOW TO CALCULATE QUICKLY: RAPID METHODS IN BASIC MATHE-MATICS, Henry Sticker. Addition, subtraction, multiplication, division, checks, etc. More than 8000 problems, solutions. 185pp. 5 × 7¼.   20295-X Pa. $2.95

THE CAT COLORING BOOK, Karen Baldauski. Handsome, realistic renderings of 40 splendid felines, from American shorthair to exotic types. 44 plates. Captions. 48pp. 8¼ × 11.   24011-8 Pa. $2.25

THE TALE OF PETER RABBIT, Beatrix Potter. The inimitable Peter's terrifying adventure in Mr. McGregor's garden, with all 27 wonderful, full-color Potter illustrations. 55pp. 4¼ × 5½. (Available in U.S. only)   22827-4 Pa. $1.75

BASIC ELECTRICITY, U.S. Bureau of Naval Personnel. Batteries, circuits, conductors, AC and DC, inductance and capacitance, generators, motors, trans-formers, amplifiers, etc. 349 illustrations. 448pp. 6½ × 9¼.   20973-3 Pa. $7.95

TOLL HOUSE TRIED AND TRUE RECIPES, Ruth Graves Wakefield. Popovers, veal and ham loaf, baked beans, much more from the famous Mass. restaurant. Nearly 700 recipes. 376pp. 5⅜ × 8½. 23560-2 Pa. $4.95

FAVORITE CHRISTMAS CAROLS, selected and arranged by Charles J.F. Cofone. Title, music, first verse and refrain of 34 traditional carols in handsome calligraphy; also subsequent verses and other information in type. 79pp. 8⅜ × 11. 20445-6 Pa. $3.50

CAMERA WORK: A PICTORIAL GUIDE, Alfred Stieglitz. All 559 illustrations from most important periodical in history of art photography. Reduced in size but still clear, in strict chronological order, with complete captions. 176pp. 8⅜ × 11¼. 23591-2 Pa. $6.95

FAVORITE SONGS OF THE NINETIES, edited by Robert Fremont. 88 favorites: "Ta-Ra-Ra-Boom-De-Aye," "The Band Played On," "Bird in a Gilded Cage," etc. 401pp. 9 × 12. 21536-9 Pa. $12.95

STRING FIGURES AND HOW TO MAKE THEM, Caroline F. Jayne. Fullest, clearest instructions on string figures from around world: Eskimo, Navajo, Lapp, Europe, more. Cat's cradle, moving spear, lightning, stars. 950 illustrations. 407pp. 5⅜ × 8½. 20152-X Pa. $5.95

LIFE IN ANCIENT EGYPT, Adolf Erman. Detailed older account, with much not in more recent books: domestic life, religion, magic, medicine, commerce, and whatever else needed for complete picture. Many illustrations. 597pp. 5⅜ × 8½. 22632-8 Pa. $7.95

ANCIENT EGYPT: ITS CULTURE AND HISTORY, J.E. Manchip White. From pre-dynastics through Ptolemies: scoiety, history, political structure, religion, daily life, literature, cultural heritage. 48 plates. 217pp. 5⅜ × 8½. (EBE) 22548-8 Pa. $4.95

KEPT IN THE DARK, Anthony Trollope. Unusual short novel about Victorian morality and abnormal psychology by the great English author. Probably the first American publication. Frontispiece by Sir John Millais. 92pp. 6½ × 9¼. 23609-9 Pa. $2.95

MAN AND WIFE, Wilkie Collins. Nineteenth-century master launches an attack on out-moded Scottish marital laws and Victorian cult of athleticism. Artfully plotted. 35 illustrations. 239pp. 6⅛ × 9¼. 24451-2 Pa. $5.95

RELATIVITY AND COMMON SENSE, Herman Bondi. Radically reoriented presentation of Einstein's Special Theory and one of most valuable popular accounts available. 60 illustrations. 177pp. 5⅜ × 8. (EUK) 24021-5 Pa. $3.95

THE EGYPTIAN BOOK OF THE DEAD, E.A. Wallis Budge. Complete reproduction of Ani's papyrus, finest ever found. Full hieroglyphic text, interlinear transliteration, word-for-word translation, smooth translation. 533pp. 6½ × 9¼. (USO) 21866-X Pa. $8.95

COUNTRY AND SUBURBAN HOMES OF THE PRAIRIE SCHOOL PERIOD, H.V. von Holst. Over 400 photographs floor plans, elevations, detailed drawings (exteriors and interiors) for over 100 structures. Text. Important primary source. 128pp. 8⅜ × 11¼. 24373-7 Pa. $5.95

SOURCE BOOK OF MEDICAL HISTORY, edited by Logan Clendening, M.D. Original accounts ranging from Ancient Egypt and Greece to discovery of X-rays: Galen, Pasteur, Lavoisier, Harvey, Parkinson, others. 685pp. 5⅜ × 8½.
20621-1 Pa. $10.95

THE ROSE AND THE KEY, J.S. Lefanu. Superb mystery novel from Irish master. Dark doings among an ancient and aristocratic English family. Well-drawn characters; capital suspense. Introduction by N. Donaldson. 448pp. 5⅜ × 8½.
24377-X Pa. $6.95

SOUTH WIND, Norman Douglas. Witty, elegant novel of ideas set on languorous Meditterranean island of Nepenthe. Elegant prose, glittering epigrams, mordant satire. 1917 masterpiece. 416pp. 5⅜ × 8½. (Available in U.S. only)
24361-3 Pa. $5.95

RUSSELL'S CIVIL WAR PHOTOGRAPHS, Capt. A.J. Russell. 116 rare Civil War Photos: Bull Run, Virginia campaigns, bridges, railroads, Richmond, Lincoln's funeral car. Many never seen before. Captions. 128pp. 9⅜ × 12¼.
24283-8 Pa. $6.95

PHOTOGRAPHS BY MAN RAY: 105 Works, 1920-1934. Nudes, still lifes, landscapes, women's faces, celebrity portraits (Dali, Matisse, Picasso, others), rayographs. Reprinted from rare gravure edition. 128pp. 9⅜ × 12¼. (Available in U.S. only)
23842-3 Pa. $7.95

STAR NAMES: THEIR LORE AND MEANING, Richard H. Allen. Star names, the zodiac, constellations: folklore and literature associated with heavens. The basic book of its field, fascinating reading. 563pp. 5⅜ × 8½. 21079-0 Pa. $7.95

BURNHAM'S CELESTIAL HANDBOOK, Robert Burnham, Jr. Thorough guide to the stars beyond our solar system. Exhaustive treatment. Alphabetical by constellation: Andromeda to Cetus in Vol. 1; Chamaeleon to Orion in Vol. 2; and Pavo to Vulpecula in Vol. 3. Hundreds of illustrations. Index in Vol. 3. 2000pp. 6⅛ × 9¼. 23567-X, 23568-8, 23673-0 Pa. Three-vol. set $36.85

THE ART NOUVEAU STYLE BOOK OF ALPHONSE MUCHA, Alphonse Mucha. All 72 plates from *Documents Decoratifs* in original color. Stunning, essential work of Art Nouveau. 80pp. 9⅜ × 12¼. 24044-4 Pa. $7.95

DESIGNS BY ERTE; FASHION DRAWINGS AND ILLUSTRATIONS FROM "HARPER'S BAZAR," Erte. 310 fabulous line drawings and 14 *Harper's Bazar* covers, 8 in full color. Erte's exotic temptresses with tassels, fur muffs, long trains, coifs, more. 129pp. 9⅜ × 12¼. 23397-9 Pa. $6.95

HISTORY OF STRENGTH OF MATERIALS, Stephen P. Timoshenko. Excellent historical survey of the strength of materials with many references to the theories of elasticity and structure. 245 figures. 452pp. 5⅜ × 8½. 61187-6 Pa. $8.95

Prices subject to change without notice.

Available at your book dealer or write for free catalog to Dept. GI, Dover Publications, Inc., 31 East 2nd St. Mineola, N.Y. 11501. Dover publishes more than 175 books each year on science, elementary and advanced mathematics, biology, music, art, literary history, social sciences and other areas.